# THE CITY OF REASON

LONDON : GEOFFREY CUMBERLEGE
OXFORD UNIVERSITY PRESS

# THE CITY OF
# REASON

BY

## SAMUEL H. BEER

ASSOCIATE PROFESSOR OF GOVERNMENT
HARVARD UNIVERSITY

GREENWOOD PRESS, PUBLISHERS
NEW YORK                    1968

LIBRARY OF CONGRESS catalogue card number: 68-23274

Printed in the United States of America

TO
R. B.

# PREFACE

In this book I have tried to state a philosophy of liberalism based on A. N. Whitehead's metaphysics of creative advance. My thesis is that man is inwardly free and, therefore, ought to be free outwardly. Man is inwardly free by virtue of his reason. Hence, the liberal ideal is a society which protects and promotes the exercise of that capacity: The City of Reason.

The book is not concerned with the form which particular institutions, political and social, might take in such a society. Rather it is concerned with the philosophical ideas which support the theory of a free society. It asks what reason is and why men ought to live by it. The answers which it suggests are derived from a Christian interpretation of Whitehead's philosophy. From that philosophy it derives a conception of reason as a method of inquiry, as an ideal of conduct, and as a kind of knowledge pointing toward the central intuitions of religious experience.

I have approached this task from a familiar problem of philosophy as it is raised anew by certain versions of modern skepticism. I have called that problem the problem of purpose. It might equally well be called the problem of irrationalism, or, even better, the problem of fatality: Why should man try to control his future and make his history in a world which seems to be governed by a blind and lawless fate? The doubt which this problem casts on many of the assumptions of science and ethics is examined and pressed home in the first two parts of the book. In developing this point I have been led to consider such matters as the problem of induction, Karl Mannheim's sociology of knowledge and John Dewey's theory of creative intelligence, as well as certain aspects of the Rousseauist, Kantian, and Hegelian theories of ethics and society, and of the Marxist philosophy of history. The third part of the book deals briefly with the problem of purpose in the light of Platonic thought and Old Testament and New Testament theology. It is principally concerned with stating the main ideas of Whitehead's philosophy of creative advance and linking them with certain theories of truth and the good which have been previously examined. The concluding chapter draws out the implications for political thought.

It is an ambitious task, perhaps too ambitious. But people will think about such questions, difficult as they may be to state clearly and answer rationally. That is grounds, I think, for trying from time to time to write about them—without dogmatism or polemic, but with as much honesty and clarity and logic as the writer has in him.

I should say, however, that the book has not been written for the professional philosopher, but for the student of political science and the general reader interested in political thought. I have approached philosophical ideas from the point of view of my own special interest, political science. Throughout I have tried to show how problems of political science continually raise classical problems of philosophy. Negatively, I have tried to show that philosophy, especially metaphysics, cannot be disregarded by the political scientist. Positively, I have tried to indicate how philosophy can be used by the political scientist, how it is relevant to his problems. So while I cannot claim that this book raises new problems or suggests new ideas, I should like to hope that it may serve as an introduction to the old but important problems of philosophy for students from a different field and readers of the present generation.

For reading the manuscript at one stage or another and for helpful criticisms, I should like to thank Raphael Demos, W. Y. Elliott, Merle Fainsod, and Henry Hart. This book is one of the Harvard Political Studies.

Samuel H. Beer

12 October 1948
Cambridge, Mass.

# CONTENTS

## INTRODUCTION

I. THE PROBLEM OF PURPOSE      I

### PART ONE
## DOUBT OF TRUTH

II. THE RELATIVITY OF TRUTH      15

III. CREATIVE INTELLIGENCE      32

### PART TWO
## DOUBT OF RIGHT

IV. THE RELATIVITY OF MORALS      51

V. THE ETHICS OF COMMUNITY      63

VI. THE ETHICS OF CIVILIZATION      79

VII. PHILOSOPHY OF HISTORY AGAINST ITSELF      91

### PART THREE
## THEODICY

VIII. ONE POWER OR MANY      111

IX. THE SEARCH FOR PURPOSE: NATURE PHILOSOPHY
AND PLATONISM      116

X. THE STRUGGLE FOR EXISTENCE: JUDAISM
AND CHRISTIANITY      125

XI. CREATIVE ADVANCE      139

XII. A SAVING ORDER      157

XIII. FAITH AND MORALS      178

## CONCLUSION

XIV. POLITICS      197

NOTES      219

# INTRODUCTION

## CHAPTER ONE

# THE PROBLEM OF
# PURPOSE

THIS IS A CREATIVE UNIVERSE AND THE HUMAN MIND IS A peculiarly creative part of it. Man's capacity to learn and, in the process of learning, to form his character is a creative power of a high order. In learning through intelligent inquiry, a man not only acquires knowledge, he also develops and extends his purposes. Knowledge does not simply lie in his mind as a reflection of fact; it becomes an instrument for changing fact. As each man's personal adventure leads him through the worlds of nature and society, new situations challenge his powers and oblige him to add to and adjust his objectives and purposes. The pursuit of truth involves the creative growth of personality.

The growth of the personality is a part of a larger process of creativity. History and nature do not simply repeat themselves over and over, but continually exhibit new forms of actuality. Not only man is creative; the universe of which he is a part also is creative. And this process of universal creativity somehow gives the creativity of man eternal meaning and lasting consequences.

For the growth of the personality is important not alone because of the internal satisfactions to which it may lead. Its essential importance lies outside man in the process of universal creativity. The creative growth of the personality fulfills a Law or Will beyond man. In recognizing this Law or Will, man gains some sense of an objective standard of ethics. He finds a duty to himself and to others. He sees, obscurely and in many shifting lights, a Higher Law which social institutions and government ought to serve. "The human psychic activity," writes Whitehead, ". . . contains the origins of precious harmonies within the transient world. The end of human society is to elicit such psychic energies."[1] Such an insight into his position in the creative universe makes man not only an intelligent animal, but also a moral animal.

In some such insight we find the ground of human rights and duties and a definition of the end of government. Yet how do we arrive at this insight? On what evidence can we base the conclusion that the world is essentially creative? For the record of history and nature and common experience shows that the world is deeply destructive as well as creative. The human psyche is the source of "precious harmonies," sometimes. Often it is the scene of jarring conflicts and the eruption of disintegrating emotions. Society is full of conflict, cruelty, frustration. History is punctuated by decline and death. Nature comes red in tooth and claw.

Judging by the record, creativity is not the law or the fundamental tendency of human nature. Within man many forces and drives compete for satisfaction besides the tendency toward intelligent inquiry. There is no reason to base our ethics on the creative tendency rather than on other different or hostile tendencies. Nor does the record entitle us to say that creativity is the law or the fundamental tendency of the social and natural worlds of which the human personality is a part. There too other forces than creative forces often triumph. In the character of universal process we can find no objective standard of ethics.

The objection, broadly stated, is that destruction, the negation of creativity, is a trait of the universe as basic as creativity. The central problem of this book is to refute this objection and to show that there is an insight, convincing to the mind and in a real sense founded on experience, which indicates that the fundamental law of the universe and of man is a law of creativity, and that in such a law we find an objective standard of ethics for man and for his social and political institutions.

*The Problem of Purpose*   The ethical problem is central, but the approach to it will be indirect. The ethical problem will be approached through another problem raised by the hypothesis that the world is fundamentally destructive, or to use a more precise word, discontinuous. If the world is discontinuous, then knowledge is in a peculiar position. For knowledge is gained from observation and experiment in a certain environment, natural and social. So far as this environment remains the same, knowledge derived from it can be used to predict and to control events in that environment. But if the environment changes, losing its familiar characteristics, of what use is the knowledge gained from experience in the previous environment?

If knowledge is to be a useful instrument of control, then the future must be like the past. So far as the world is destructive and discontinuous, the future will not be like the past. In a discontinuous world, instrumental knowledge, that is, knowledge which has become purpose, is of dubious value. Our plans and purposes may have their expected consequences. They also may have consequences totally unexpected and even hostile to what we had intended. This is the problem of purpose through which the argument of this book will approach the ethical problem.

The problem of purpose is not the ethical problem. It confronts us whether or not we care about standards of ethics or justice. People frequently dismiss the ethical problem as hopeless or meaningless. To search for an objective standard of ethics, they say, involves the student in metaphysics and religion; but these matters are matters of opinion, not reason and experience, and the student committed to the methods of intelligent inquiry should dismiss the ethical problem from his researches.

Of course, they continue, men do cherish certain "values";

men feel strongly about certain principles of individual conduct and social organization. It happens that our society is
fairly well agreed on a certain set of values. No reason can
be given for preferring one set of values to another, so the
task of the student of society or politics is not to look for
such a nonexistent reason, but rather to find means for protecting and realizing these accepted values. Here is his great
task: To find through observation and experiment more efficient means for achieving these given ends. To extend knowledge in order that the consequences of social action may be
brought more and more under our control and history made
more and more the result of our plans.

Such an approach leads directly to the problem of purpose.
For it raises the question, What reason have we for thinking
that we can control events and plan our history? Why may
we believe that knowledge is, or can be, an instrument for
controlling the consequences of our acts?

When the student of politics and society considers recent
history, he may be ready to grant that there is some doubt
about the answer to this question. Human efforts to understand and control history have gained some great successes.
But these successes have been matched, or more than matched,
by hideous failure. Our world has suffered disasters as crushing as those of a far more primitive and ignorant age. When
we look around us, we see a world we never made; which no
one made, but which seems to have sprung from an alien
and inexplicable fate.

Wars, depressions, the confused struggle of classes, the ir-
reconcilable fears and ambitions of states: these things have
produced a history which no man has desired and which is
strange and bitter to all men. There is no lack of counselors
who claim to understand the real reasons for such events
and to have plans which will prevent them. But the analysts
and planners quarrel violently among themselves. The confusion of events is confounded by the confusion of counsel.

Yet the social and political scientist does not despair. The record of the social sciences may not provide a defense of the instrumental value of knowledge. But in the natural sciences surely it is a different story. Here we must find an instance of knowledge which has achieved certainty, that is, which really can lead to the consequences which it predicts.

But do we? Do the logician and student of scientific method give us a satisfying defense of the instrumental value of knowledge? This question will be considered more extensively in the next chapter, but here we shall discuss it briefly, for it enables us to restate the problem of purpose. The problem of purpose can be stated as that familiar problem of philosophy, the problem of induction or prediction. Given the fact that I have seen a certain connection between events in the past, what justifies me in assuming that this connection will hold in the future? I have seen *B* follow *A*. Why, when I again see *A*, may I infer that *B* will follow? If this inference is sensible, then human purpose is sensible. For I may now confidently use my knowledge of the connections of events in the past in order to develop plans and purposes which will control the future.

This is the problem of purpose in the simplest form. But stating the problem in simplest form does not make its solution any more evident. The student of methodology finds that sometimes the connections which have been observed in the past also hold good in the future. And that sometimes they do not. In some cases, predictions founded on past experience are borne out, and sometimes they are not. Hence, he will reject with some vehemence the suggestion that any knowledge is "certain" and will insist that all knowledge is "contingent." He will not speak of the "laws of nature" but of "the working hypotheses of science." And in any concrete situation he will carefully refrain from making any promise that such an hypothesis will actually work. For he has discovered what everyday experience and the record of planners and statesmen continually confirm: that sometimes men get what they plan and work for, and sometimes not. "The events of the future," writes Wittgenstein, "*cannot* be inferred from those of the present. Superstition is the belief in the causal nexus."[2]

The philosopher may press the argument further. He may argue that this very examination of the past in order to discern the future itself assumes what we want to prove. Knowledge is what is known; it refers to observed fact. But the future, the real future approaching a man here and now, can never be a part of observed fact. So regardless of what past experience tells us about the success or failure of our predictions, we may not infer from it any conclusions about their success or failure in the future.

Such a refined argument, when developed, is convincing, but it is not likely to carry much weight with active, purposive men. The really difficult fact is that, according to the record, men have often found the future to be quite unlike the past. And in truth, if the future had always been like the past, it is not likely that even philosophers would have dared suggest their more refined argument. It is not likely they would have thought of it. The root of our problem is not the speculations of philosophers but the changeability of the world. Here is why, in the words of Whitehead, "the theory of Induction is the despair of philosophy."[3]

The problem of purpose is a problem not of the social sciences, alone, but of all science, of all knowledge which is held to be a means of controlling events. Whether or not you are concerned with ethics you must face this problem.

*Irrationalism*    The trouble appears at first to be our ignorance. If only we knew more, it seems, then we should be able to control events. But when we reflect further we see that our ignorance would be no handicap, if only the environment in which we work were stable and continuous from moment to moment. It is only when the environment, social or natural, changes that our ignorance leads us into false expectations.

Indeed, part of the instability of the environment comes from man himself, from the consequences, intended and unintended, of his attempts to plan his future and control nature. Human ambition itself is a principle violator of the rule of stability without which that ambition can never have any certain gratification.

The difficulty is that the world is destructive, discontinuous. If we follow our experience and what we know of the experience of the race, we shall conclude that every stable thing or order will sooner or later be extinguished. Individual men die; so do social systems, nations, races, and species of living creatures. Planets age, suns are exhausted, and stars, it has been said, explode. Every order of existence which we have investigated has shown itself to be mortal.

The inevitable perishing of things is the root of our problem. For if every order of things must perish, it follows that someday any system of knowledge founded upon such an order must become outmoded. We do not know when the order represented by our present knowledge will come to an end. Obviously, our knowledge itself cannot tell us that. We only know that it will surely come to an end. We do not know when our knowledge will be outmoded, nor when its calculations will prove false. It may be tomorrow. It may not be for many years. All we know is that sooner or later these calculations will fail, because sooner or later all things fail.

Various names might be given to the general view of the world which these paragraphs have tried to suggest. It might be called pluralism or relativism or the philosophy of the flux. In this book it will also be called irrationalism, since this term serves to connect that view more emphatically with the problem of purpose.

The term irrationalism is used so loosely that it is impossible to find a single definition which holds of all uses of the term. Very commonly the term is used to refer to the influence of emotion on human conduct. A man has some plan of action he is trying to follow; some emotion interferes, diverting him from his intended course. So far as he is diverted from following his plan, we say his action is irrational. A judge intends to decide a case on the basis of evidence and law, but unconscious motives or social prejudice prevent him from seeing the law and the facts in the proper perspective and thereby make his decision irrational.

Consider two other examples: A department of government administration draws up an organizational chart defining the functions of its subdivisions. This is the plan to be followed. But in practice the influence of personalities, conflicting interests of subordinates, and similar forces prevent the department from operating rationally, that is, according to plan. Again: a national society develops an analysis of economic process which substantially explains events and enables the nation to increase its wealth; for example, the modified system of *laisser faire* accepted by the American people and their governments before 1929. Then an unexpected catastrophe such as the Great Depression brutally disappoints well-established expectations and involves events quite at variance with the traditional economic analysis. To the members of this society, the processes of the economy are irrational; they do not follow the accepted plan.

In the last two examples, the irrationality of events does not arise from the influence of emotion. But in these examples as in the first two, the connection with the problem of purpose is obvious. There is a plan, based upon knowledge of how to accomplish some end. That plan is disrupted by intervening forces and the expected consequences fail to be achieved. The process is not continuous, but discontinuous. The irrationality of events in each case lies in their discontinuity.

The problem of purpose does not arise simply because man is irrational. Not only man is irrational; the world is irrational. Things come into existence, continue for a time, then go out of existence. Between their histories there is little or no connection. They are separate, plural, discontinuous. There is no whole which makes sense of them all; there is no general plan or law which rules them and puts each in its place. In short, we live not in a universe, but in a multiverse.[4]

The purpose of this book is to refute irrationalism. The thesis of this book is that the world is rational: it is a universe which joins in real togetherness all the manifold pluralities of history and nature. In such an insight into the ultimate rational nature of things we find a Law of Reason which is an ethical imperative for man and a solution to the problem of purpose.

*Defeatism* That view of the world which we have called irrationalism raises an important problem of theory. It also creates a practical problem. Irrationalism is a counsel of despair and, if accepted, will in some measure affect the way men behave. If men seriously believe that they cannot control their fate, this belief will affect what they do to control that fate. They will become defeatists, distrusting plans, not because of the demerit of this or that plan, but simply because they are human plans. The subject of this book is the arguments of irrationalism, not its effects. However, we may digress for a moment to speculate on the ways irrationalism may affect practice.

In a sense, men cannot avoid planning. If you reject a certain proposed plan, you are left with the expectations and purposes on which you were previously acting. You are still acting as if certain behavior in the present would lead to certain consequences in the future. The irrationalist would not deny this. He would merely say that these expectations are arbitrary and senseless. Man cannot really control his fate, but he tries to. That, as cynics have often said, is one of the things which makes him so amusing to watch.

Yet even if men do not give up all purpose, the virus of irrationalism tends to prevent them from doing their best. In practice, its views assail any but the most ingrained expectations and hold people back from acting on the widest knowledge available to them.

In his daily life a man decides what he will do with the help of a great mass of expectations. He expects that a certain line of ambulation will take him to the bus-stop; that a certain procedure before a court will enable him to recover a bad debt; that going to college will help him get a better job. These expectations give him a picture of how his society works. They tell him what he can count on happening as the consequences of his acts in the context of that society. They constitute his perspective of the institutions, habits, and customs of his society. In an age of security, these expectations are substantially borne out. The individual tends to conclude that they describe the whole working of that society.

In an age of insecurity, these expectations are often disappointed. Frustration, the shock of events alone, will lead him to distrust these expectations. Here is the beginning of defeatism. The effect of irrationalism is to reinforce his doubts and to give him what may rather facetiously be called a rationalization of the world's irrationality. It discourages him from relying upon expectations founded upon any but the simpler and more automatic calculations. Any attempt to go beyond these calculations and to provide for a more distant object by a more complex plan at every step meets the doubt that human purpose cannot control events.

In modern society, coöperation between many groups and classes involves complex planning. It is not immediately clear to a group just what benefits will come to it from supporting, and from compromising with, the many other groups seeking benefits along with it. Only a complex calculation can show the group how in the long run it will benefit. But if the doubts of irrationalism are at work, the group will have little will to make, and to act on, this complex calculation. Each group will tend to look only to its interests in the immediate future, distrusting not so much the good will as the competence of its society and government to provide long-run benefits. So, from the doubts of irrationalism may proceed a distrust of other groups, a splitting up of society into factions, a clamor for special advantage and a refusal to coöperate. Hopelessness and social strife will be encouraged by irrationalism. Yet if one tendency is to exacerbate distrust, another tendency of this monster of self-contradiction is to lead to acts of fatuous trustfulness. For if the world is irrational, it makes very little difference what you do or whom you trust. "Anything," as Mussolini once said, "is possible, even the most impossible and most senseless." [5]

Irrationalism, therefore, may lead you to entertain absurd expectations; indeed, so far as possible, to give up altogether expectations and attempts to understand. You do not try to understand what you are doing. You merely do as you are told. You are bound to your leaders, not by understanding and common expectations, but by blind feeling. You are similar to your fellow instruments, not because you and they think alike—you don't think—but because you feel the same inexplicable impulses to subordination.

We ridicule and despise the man who yields to irrationalism. Yet in his despair we touch a feeling deeply involved with the current of doubt and skepticism which runs through the thinking of many of us today. For instance, in political matters, what the modern doubter distrusts is not so much the government's morals, as its competence. What he cannot avoid thinking is that these well-laid plans, whether a "raid on the Treasury" or a high-minded pursuit of the more abundant life, are just as likely to produce strange and unwanted results as they are to accomplish their declared aims.

Suppose we find a defeatist who is also a moral skeptic. Suppose we restore to him a fervent belief in the ends of democracy and the morals of the Sermon on the Mount. Will that not leave him just as ineffective and even more miserable? For now he will aspire to accomplish these ends, yet distrust any suggested means. He will long to work for Freedom and Peace, but he will not be able to tell what kind of career, what kind of war, what party policy will genuinely give him the chance. He will want to be good, high-minded and patriotic, but not know how.

This more miserable condition, it seems to me, is closer to the state of mind of the modern doubter than the simpler and commoner picture of a man sunk in selfish appetite and deaf to the appeal of idealism. And in some measure we all share his mood. We long for the good, solid world of our fathers, along with the improvements which their ideals have suggested. Yet we wonder how to make this world and how to avoid losing what we already have of it and whether such an aim is within human power.

### PART ONE

# DOUBT OF TRUTH

## CHAPTER TWO

# THE RELATIVITY OF
# TRUTH

IN THIS CHAPTER THE PROBLEM OF PURPOSE WILL BE STATED
and discussed in the light of familiar problems of social science
and philosophy. The importance of the problem to any thinking man will appear and at the same time the manner in which
any formulation of the problem continually raises larger problems of metaphysics. The following 'chapter will turn to
another statement of the problem emerging from a review
of John Dewey's analysis of experience. The problem of purpose will be the central concern, but in Dewey's analysis elements of a solution to the ethical problem will also be found.

Part II of the book will be primarily concerned with a claim
of ethical theory to solve our problem. We shall find there
not a solution, but the hint of a solution. In Part III, after
some of the classical attempts to solve our problem have been
considered, a solution will be worked out on the basis of
A. N. Whitehead's philosophy of creative advance.

*Perspective and Interpretation*  We begin with certain ideas
developed by Karl Mannheim in his *Ideology and Utopia*.
These ideas are a good starting-point because they lead to a
statement of the problem of purpose as a problem of social
science and control. Mannheim is acutely aware of the fact that
our science of society is inadequate to the problems of our
society. His statement of the reasons for this inadequacy is
thoughtful and penetrating. His proposed solution, while not
solving the underlying problem, leads to a better understanding of it.

In *Ideology and Utopia* Mannheim develops his notion of

a new social science, the sociology of knowledge. He shows that in modern society men from different classes and groups look at the same events differently. Apart from any intention to deceive or distort, the bias of his class or group leads one man to understand events differently from the way they are understood by a man from another group and, consequently, to make different predictions concerning them.

This difference between men Mannheim calls a difference of perspective, "thought-style," or *Weltanschauung*. When men with different perspectives look at the same events or situations they will see different "facts." They will see different facts because, in the first place, a man's view of the facts always contains some interpretation of them; some understanding of their possible consequences or meaning. In the second place, this interpretation will spring from the knowledge which he brings to his observation. What he sees in certain events will depend, not only on those events, but also on what he has already been led to believe events of this kind lead to and are associated with. His knowledge will be largely determined by his class or group; hence, the interpretation which he inseparably connects with the facts will be different from the interpretation put on the facts by a man of another class or group.

Mannheim insists that the "facts" are not simply "given." An integral and inseparable part of a fact is the interpretation which a man gives to that fact and which, indeed, guides him in selecting what he regards as fact. To appeal to experience is not to appeal to a single, unambiguous criterion which all men must agree on. Quite the contrary. Men with different perspectives will have different "experiences." They will be looking for different facts and what they find will be different. The problem, to use terms loosely, is not that one must choose either empiricism or apriorism. It is rather that one cannot get an empiricism that is free of apriori assumptions.

"No one," writes Mannheim, "denies the possibility of empirical research, nor does anyone maintain that facts do not exist. We, too, appeal to 'facts' for our proof, but the question of the nature of facts is in itself a considerable problem. They exist for the mind always in an intellectual and social context. That they can be understood and formulated implies already the existence of a conceptual apparatus. And if this conceptual apparatus is the same for all the members of a group, the presuppositions (i.e. the possible social and intellectual values) which underlie the individual concepts, never become perceptible. The somnambulistic certainty that has existed with reference to the problem of truth during stable periods of history thus becomes intelligible. However, once the unanimity is broken, the fixed categories which used to give experience its reliable and coherent character undergo an inevitable disintegration. There arise divergent and conflicting modes of thought which (unknown to the thinking subject) order the same facts of experience into different systems of thought, and cause them to be perceived through different categories."[1]

*Perspective and Interest*  Mannheim is saying, then, that what a man holds to be the "facts" will invariably contain some interpretation springing from his knowledge. Furthermore, he argues that this interpretation will be deeply affected by a man's interests. All perspectives, as he puts it, are "interest-bound."

This connection of interest and interpretation arises simply from the way knowledge itself is gained. It does not come from something which interferes with learning, such as a "bad" or selfish will. It lies in the very nature of learning. To put it briefly: A man learns about the world by trying to get what he wants in it. Hence, what he knows, so far as he knows anything, is how to get things that he wants and how to avoid things he doesn't want. He has got this knowledge in the past while trying to satisfy his wants and interests. So what it tells him about the present facts is, more or less inadequately, how they can satisfy or threaten those interests.

This states the position crudely. There is one qualification which Mannheim's views require us to make immediately. It is that a man's interests are emphatically social interests. That is, they are interests which he has in common with other people, his class, party, nation, or even his age. He is born into a group and inherits the interests and perspective of that group. His knowledge is gained, not merely from his own direct experience, but also indirectly from the experience of his group. It is knowledge, not merely of what touches his personal interest, but also of those consequences which his group has come to recognize as favorable or unfavorable to its interests. His interpretation of events is "interest-bound." But that does not mean that he thinks of their meaning only for himself as opposed to all other individuals. Rather he interprets these events with knowledge which has been gained by his group in the pursuit of its interests and he acts with his group in the further pursuit of these interests.

A principal feature of the sociology of knowledge, writes Mannheim, is "that it does not sever the concretely existing modes of thought from the context of collective action through which we first discover the world in an intellectual sense. Men living in groups do not merely coexist physically as discrete individuals. They do not confront the objects of the world from the abstract levels of a contemplating mind as such, nor do they do so exclusively as solitary beings. On the contrary, they act with and against one another in diversely organized groups and while doing so they think with and against one another. These persons, bound together into groups, strive in accordance with the character and position of the groups to which they belong to change the surrounding world of nature and society or attempt to maintain it in a given condition. It is the direction of this will to change or to maintain, of this collective activity, which produces the guiding thread for the emergence of their problems, their concepts and their forms of thought. In accord with the particular context of collective activity in which they participate, men always tend to see the world which surrounds them differently."[2]

Mannheim illustrates his theory copiously. In order to give point to his generalizations, we may consider one of his examples. Among the five types of perspective which he distinguishes in modern society, one is that of "bureaucratic conservatism." The tendency of this kind of thought is to turn all problems of politics into problems of administration. Like everyone else, the bureaucrat has learned through doing, and all he and his group have done is to administer. Hence, when he discovers, for instance, that a law is not being executed, the only causes and remedies which occur to him are concerned with the technique of administration. He does not see the forces which bring laws into existence, nor those which help or hinder their execution, outside the realm of administration.

"It is therefore no wonder," writes Mannheim, "that in every revolution the bureaucracy tries to find a remedy by means of arbitrary decrees rather than to meet the political situation on its own grounds. . . Every bureaucracy . . . in accord with the peculiar emphasis on its own position, tends to generalize its own experience and to overlook the fact that the realm of administration and smoothly functioning order represents only a part of the total political reality."[3]

Like other analysts and planners, the bureaucratic conservative, in Justice Holmes's memorable phrase, takes the familiar for the universal. We can hardly blame him for this. He is acting empirically, that is, on calculations founded on experience. That experience is partial. But we cannot ask him to wait until he knows everything.

*A Science of the Social Whole*  We need not accept Mannheim's analysis of the bureaucratic mind, nor the other items in his taxonomy of modern social thought, in order to see that he is getting at a very important problem. The point that he brings out is that there are many ways of approaching social and political problems today and that each approach is one-sided, seeing only some of the real possibilities. Each, therefore, is unreliable as a guide to successful action.

We are used to seeing historians disagree over the causes of great events in the past—the fall of the Roman Empire, the crusades, the Reformation, the French Revolution. And we feel it is the part of intelligence to grant that probably none of these disagreements will ever be resolved by a single, generally accepted account. When we examine events of the more recent past, such as World War I or the Great Depression, we find the same sort of disagreement. Regarding these disagreements we find it more disturbing to make the same admission. For the problems of preventing world war and world depression are still very much with us. It seems we must solve them or perish. Yet if our experts argue with as little hope of agreement as the historians, we lack even a firm starting-point for our plans and remedies.

It is a painfully familiar fact. The experts often enough claim to be disinterested. And often enough we can clear them of any charge of dishonesty or willful deception. Yet each seems to think in accord with certain "inarticulate major premises" which he shares with some group. When compared with those who disagree with him, each is a partisan. Politics is not the creation of politicians. If Congress, as one writer has observed, were composed exclusively of social scientists, it would still be a political body, parties and blocs would arise, and controversy would be no less bitter than at present.[4] The experts, objective as they may try to be, are partisan and when we try to choose between them, we find ourselves becoming partisan. We try to check the conflicting plans and analyses against the lessons of our own experience. But this experience itself is partial and springs in great measure from our class or national background. So, in spite of the most disinterested will, we are led to side with the champions of that group which largely shares and determines our own experience.

The facts seem so plain to each side: That the working man can be free and prosperous only under a system of free private enterprise. That Labor can progress only if it uses government to enforce its rights. That saving what is left of private enterprise requires a balanced budget—or an unbalanced budget. That wars spring from the internal contradictions of finance capitalism and can be prevented only by the abolition of that system. That wars can be prevented if nations will recognize their paramount common interest in peace.

Each side appeals to experience. Each documents its arguments and plans. To each the facts are so plain and self-evident that it is no wonder it can understand the opposition of the others only as the machinations of an evil will. But when a man for a moment surveys the bedlam of social controversy as a whole, he may begin to wonder whether there are any such evil wills, whether all parties are not equally dupes of their own partiality. But that road of reflection leads straight to cynicism.

Cynicism is one road, the road of the irrationalist and the defeatist. There is another likely reflection. When we see partial truths at war, we may suggest that they be brought together, in order that the whole truth may emerge. To many of us, this is the value of parliamentary assemblies, within nations and between nations. We hope that in discussion the champions of partial truths will learn from one another and that reason, the whole truth, will prevail.

Substantially, this is Mannheim's proposal. The task of the sociology of knowledge, he writes, is to bring together in a single system the various perspectives and systems of knowledge which we find in modern society. It should embrace the segment of truth revealed by each, and so raise our knowledge toward a "total comprehension" of society.

In this way, according to Mannheim, a new kind of objectivity will be attained in our science of society. For that science will then be free of the bias and subjectivity of the views of different schools of thought. Yet it will embrace the truth which the partial views contain. In practical terms, this means that the views of the new science will have greater probability and man will be farther along the road to the total control of society, which, indeed, Mannheim thinks is a not-far-distant goal. When that goal is reached, we shall have a true science of society, "a science of the whole."[5]

*Doubt of Mannheim's Solution*   This is an agreeable thought. But does it follow from what Mannheim has said? He has shown that there have arisen many different ways of looking at the same facts. May we not infer that there remain a good many more possible ways of looking at them? He has shown that different groups see different possibilities in the same facts. Can we conclude that there are no more possibilities, or only a few, which have not yet been seen? Indeed, if the future is to be like the past, there must remain new perspectives, new systems of possibility, which have not yet emerged. And if there are many more possibilities which we have not yet seen and which would not be comprehended even by the proposed synthesis of all known perspectives, then will not the predictions of our new science, like those of the old, remain at the mercy of forces not yet understood?

Let us suppose that the principles of the various perspectives could be combined in a single consistent system—a very doubtful supposition. It will then be true that the predictions of this new system will be founded upon a larger set of principles. In relation to the predictions of the constituent perspectives, they will be "the most probable." But how probable will they be in relation to all possibilities, unknown as well as known? What counts is not whether we know more than we did yesterday, or whether we know more than someone else, but whether we know enough to cope with the world. The measure of our strength is not the weakness of others, but the tasks which the world sets us.

There is, it seems to me, an extraordinary assumption underlying Mannheim's proposal—"an inarticulate major premise," if you like. It comes to something like this: That it is possible for men to know everything. It is the notion that in some sense the sum of things which can actually happen in nature and society, the real possibilities, have a limit which we approach as our science grows.

He seems to say as much in sentences like the following: "the sphere of the rationalizable and of the rationally controllable (even in our most personal life) is always growing, while the sphere of the irrational becomes correspondingly narrower."[6] He seems to be saying here that, as our knowledge of the real possibilities grows, it approaches the limit of what can happen in the world. Hence, the ratio between our knowledge and all possible knowledge increases. And our power over nature and the probability of our predictions also grows.

But what grounds can one find for this assumption? Granting that our knowledge does grow, it remains that the world itself is continually changing, continually giving us new objects to investigate and to learn to control. Is this not precisely what Mannheim's study of "ideologies" tells us? This term he applies to those perspectives which, growing up in an earlier period of a society, fail to work when that society changes. The truth of an "ideology" was relative to a certain time and place. Can any truth, even the truth of Mannheim's proposed synthesis of perspectives, escape relativity?

Society will not patiently stand still while the experimenter works on it, gradually extending his knowledge to embrace all its important features. History is full of surprises. It is creative. It is destructive. Simply for our knowledge to grow is not enough to assure us that our power over nature and society is growing. Indeed, we are lucky if that steady growth enables us to maintain our power at its old level. As the Red Queen said to Alice in a work by a profound student of irrationalism, we must go twice that fast to get anywhere.

When a man finds that his knowledge includes and goes

beyond the knowledge of other men, he concludes that his plans and predictions are "the most probable." To say that his knowledge is "the most probable" is permissible only in a limited sense. It is permissible only if it is taken to mean simply that his knowledge embraces a wider system of principles than the knowledge of the others. The question of what will happen in the future; of what the plans of this man or party will actually lead to, is still undetermined. He will be a little vain if he assumes that because no man present can refute his arguments, they are irrefutable.

*The Root of Perspective*   Let us restate and generalize some of the points of the argument. At first, it appears that the root of perspective and the partiality of knowledge is desire, class interest, or some form of selfish willing. What makes a man's knowledge biased, it seems, is that he is interested in how the the situation which he is observing will turn out. The way for him to get rid of this limitation, it follows, is to cleanse himself of interest in the outcome of events, i.e., become a disinterested observer. Apparently this is in Mannheim's mind when he says that the social scientist is interested in the outcome of the processes which he describes and, therefore, cannot look at those processes impartially.[7] Believing this, you might distinguish between the natural and social sciences by holding that the natural scientist can look at his object impartially while the social scientist cannot.

No doubt, students of social problems are often moved by partisan feeling, even when they think they are being impartial. Probably unconscious motives sometimes lead them to overlook what others regard as obvious facts, or to draw unwarranted conclusions from observed facts. Very likely partisan feeling and unconscious motives affect the thought of social scientist more than they do the thought of natural scientists.

But the discussion of Mannheim's views has revealed a deeper root of perspective. All knowledge is affected, whether the knowledge of the natural scientist, the social scientist, or the man of everyday, practical affairs. To put it bluntly, the difficulty is that men cannot know everything. The individual student has learned to look for and identify certain kinds of facts and connections of facts. His knowledge may grow. He may associate himself with others in a common effort to solve problems. It remains that what he or his group expects and looks for in the world is a fractional selection of all the things the world can make and do. Here is the root of his partiality and fallibility. Here is at once the source and the expression of his finitude.

Consider the position of the student trying to discover a necessary sequence between antecedents and consequents in some process of the natural or social worlds. He finds that a certain antecedent, $A$, is regularly followed by a certain consequent, $B$. Let us suppose he establishes a carefully controlled situation in which he has made note of every factor which could affect the outcome of the process. Let us suppose that he then introduces the particular antecedent, $A$, into this situation and finds that now, and only now, the consequent, $B$, appears. Since by our supposition no other factor has been introduced into the situation except $A$, and since $B$ appears only upon the introduction of $A$, may the student not infer that there is a causal or necessary connection between $A$ and $B$?

According to John Stuart Mill, the student could make this inference. The procedure of experimentation outlined above, Mill named the Method of Difference[8] and celebrated as that "canon of induction" which would give "rigorous certainty"[9] to the discovery of causal laws. Yet the difficulties which arise in practice are easy to see and have often been pointed out. The principal one arises from the original supposition. How can the student be sure that he has made note of every factor which could affect the outcome? How can he be certain that he has not overlooked some factor which his training has not taught him to look for, or which his techniques make it impossible for him to observe? How can he be sure that it was not such an unknown which was responsible for the appearance of the consequent, $B$?[10] Of course, he will from time to time discover new factors which are relevant to his experiments: that is one way his science progresses. But should not that experience itself lead him to expect that there are more unknowns yet to be found? So long as there do remain unknown factors, the inquirer who is seeking to learn how to control events is limited in what he observes by the perspective given him by his training and experience. In short, by his ignorance.

Yet in a sense ignorance would be no great handicap if only the world would remain the same. That is, if the environment of the student's experiments and observations would remain the same, then even if he did not know all the conditions which had a real part in producing a certain result, he could nevertheless be certain that the environment would provide them. In such a stable and unvarying environment, if he repeated a certain operation, then surely the same result would follow as before.

The presupposition is that the future will be like the past. That is, that the operations of the experimenter or planner will be the same as in the past and that they will be conducted in a similar environment. If this were the case, we could be persuaded that the experimenter or planner would find his expectations, founded on previous experience, borne out in the future.

Sometimes this presupposition substantially corresponds to fact. To take an example from the social sciences: In the United States for a considerable period the "laws" of price formation developed by laisser-faire economists were substantially verified by the actual operations of the economy.[11] Then as oligopoly rose and competition declined in many sectors of the economy, the facts departed farther and farther from these "laws." As the epoch of laisser-faire drew to a close, new hypotheses had to be developed to describe the process of price formation.[12]

Presupposing that a certain social epoch will continue, we may conclude that the knowledge founded on experience during that epoch will tend to be borne out by experience. Whitehead holds that a similar but more general presupposition is needed to justify induction of any kind. He states this presupposition in his theory of cosmic epochs. "In every inductive judgment," he writes, "there is . . . contained a presupposition of the maintenance of the general order of the immediate environment, so far as concerns actual entities within the scope of the induction. The inductive judgment has regard to the statistical probabilities inherent in this given order. The anticipations are devoid of meaning apart from the definite cosmic order which they presuppose."[13]

The difficulty is that the presupposition that a certain epoch, social or cosmic, will continue is simply a presupposition. Our knowledge is founded on observation and experiment during a certain epoch. Knowledge which describes connections within this epoch obviously cannot tell us when or how that epoch will come to an end and when those connections will no longer be exemplified in fact. We may push our study farther and examine how one epoch goes out of existence and another comes into existence, as we study history in order to elicit the "laws" of social evolution or culture change. But the same problem presents itself. These "laws" are themselves general characteristics of an epoch embracing that course of events within which these "laws" apply. Such "laws" cannot tell us when that epoch will end and the "laws" themselves cease to apply. Unlike Baron Munchausen we cannot pull ourselves out of this bog with our own hands.

*Probability* Perspective springs from ignorance, that is, from the fact that our observations of situations in society and nature cannot be exhaustive. The evils of perspective, the failures and frustrations of human purpose, spring from the changeability of the world. In whatever subtle guise we mask it, the supposition that the future will be like the past is crude and incredible.[14] From moment to moment, each man faces a future which he cannot in any respect control with certainty.

Perhaps this is the trouble: we are crying for the moon of certainty. Are we not, like Mill, trying to make of knowledge a set of laws which invariably correspond to fact? Must we not grant, as the critics of Mill insist, that empirical knowledge, whether gained through the rigorous inductive methods of science, or the looser methods of practical common sense, can never be certain, but only probable? Is this not the solution to the problem of purpose which the sensible man will content himself with; namely, that we can never say that our attempts to control events will certainly succeed, but only that they probably will?[15]

Probability is one of the more confused notions of philosophy.[16] One use of the term appears to be easy to understand and quite in accord with common sense usage. For instance, let us suppose that mortality statistics show that of all males in the United States who live to the age of thirty, one-fifth die before reaching the age of forty. Assuming this is the only relevant information we have, we may then say that the probability that any particular thirty-year-old man will die before he reaches forty is one in five, or 20 per cent. Or, putting it another way, we may say that if the statement, "He will live until he is forty," were applied to every man in the United States who became thirty today, this statement would prove to be true in four-fifths of all cases. We could not be certain that this statement would be true in any particular case, but we would believe that in the long run, that is, within ten years, the statistical law that four-fifths would live would be borne out.

The example is highly simplified, but it illustrates one use of the term probability familiar in everyday planning and calculation. We find in experience that a certain property occurs among the members of a class in a certain proportion. We predict that this property will characterize members of that class in the future, not certainly, but with greater or less probability, according as that proportion is large or small. The statistical probability may be stated with mathematical precision, or in vague terms such as "very likely," "hardly probable," "barely possible." Should not a sensible man be content with knowledge of such probabilities? Such knowledge cannot tell him with certainty what will happen in any particular situation. But may he not believe that "in the long run" the chances will mature and he will profit more than if he had relied on improbabilities?

The argument has an obvious difficulty which illustrates another sense of the term probability. Suppose that in our experience we have found that a certain property has been invariably connected with the members of a certain class of entities. May we then infer that the probability of its being connected with such entities in the future is 100 per cent, in other words, certain? We may not, although common sense is strongly inclined to. Even if experience has shown the connection to be invariable, the prediction still has only probability.

Universal confirmation of a proposition in the past does not make the proposition certain in the future.[17] Nor does a partial confirmation make it certain that the proposition will be confirmed in the future in the same proportion. Consider again the example of the statistical law of mortality of thirty-year-old males. Given the "law" that four-fifths of the thirty-year-old males will live to be forty, it follows that the probability that any one will do so is 80 per cent. But we must note that this "law" itself is only probable. It is not certain that four-fifths of any class of thirty-year-old United States males will actually live to see forty. War, pestilence, a revolution in preventive medicine, changes in the economy or climate—to name only a few possibilities—could make the "law" utterly useless and out of conformity with the facts. This "law" reflects the statistical probabilities inherent in a certain social epoch. Any serious change in the character of this epoch can make the "law" obsolete.

But how can a man act without certainty of some kind? He chooses between alternative lines of conduct, guided by his knowledge of probabilities. But why should he follow this knowledge unless he is certain that "in the long run," "in most cases," "by and large," the more probable events will occur? He makes this effort, he expends this energy, for the sake of results. He is ready to put up with failure from time to time; indeed, he expects it. But what is the point in making this effort of thought and action, unless he really knows, that is, is certain,[18] that ultimately and in the balance his knowledge of probabilities will get him the results he aims at? If his knowledge of probabilities is merely the reflection of the past, if it tells him nothing about the future, then it would appear that he is wasting a good deal of energy and living in a world of illusion.

A sense of the illusory quality of purpose and planning clings to the word "probable" along with the statistical sense. We say that even generalizations with 100 per cent confirmation are still not certain, but only probable. One thing we are trying to express is our knowledge that unpredictable contingencies from time to time can, and do, upset the most familiar rules and expectations. Any man's perspective on fact is derived from a limited area of experience. By communication with others he may widen his perspective and extend vicariously the area of his experience. But if he is to control the future, he must command the whole realm of possibility[19].

In this sense, probable means "it seems," "in my opinion," "apparently." The word refers to a contrast between "seeming" and "being," between "opinion" and "truth," between "appearance" and "reality." This contrast is the source of some of the principal problems of metaphysics. The problem of purpose is: Why should a man or a group or a state try to use his or its knowledge to control the future, if there is no certainty that in the long run such an attempt will lead to more favorable results? This statement of the problem expands into larger problems. The problem of purpose cannot be solved solely in terms of logic and methodology.[20] It continually forces the mind to consider larger questions of the nature of the universe and of human destiny.

It would be a relief to be able to disregard the problem of purpose. As seekers of knowledge, we should be relieved to be able to call it a "pseudo-problem" and with the positivists to confine our attention to observing correlations of fact without hazarding predictions about the future. As men of practical activity, we should be glad to forget the future and with the cynics to live for the present alone. But can you disregard the problem? Can you avoid trying to look ahead and guiding your present conduct by what you think you see? Can you at the same time eradicate the overarching doubt that you live in a world of illusion which at any moment may be shattered by the irruption of a reality utterly foreign to your plans and expectations?

It is a hellish predicament. As Burns said in his great poem on planning addressed to a mouse:

> Still thou art blest compar'd wi' me!
> The present only toucheth thee:
> But, Och! I backward cast my e'e,
>     On prospects drear!
> An' forward, tho' I canna see,
>     I guess and fear.

## CHAPTER THREE

# CREATIVE INTELLIGENCE

JOHN DEWEY IS A FRIEND OF PLANNING AND OF HUMAN PUR-
pose. No one could have stronger sympathies with our efforts
to control nature and to make the world a better place. In his
works he analyzes the process of purposive action with penetrating insight and a faithful regard for the facts. Yet this very
effort to give full credit to the powers of intelligence leaves one
feeling that his fundamental irrationalism is almost insuper-
able. He shows how, in a senseless world, there is often sense
and progress. But for Dewey, as for his master, James, that
world remains in the end senseless and blind.

*The Skeptic's Argument* What Dewey asserts[1] can be approached by contrasting it with what he denies. Like any
sensible man he denies the arguments of the philosophical
skeptic. It may not seem very important to find that he makes
this denial. The views of the skeptic are so offensive to common sense that it seems no one but a pedant could concern
himself with them.

Yet the arguments of the skeptic are important. They are
important because of the counterarguments to which one
must resort in order to refute them and establish common
sense. For in order to rationalize and defend what is common
and accepted, one must resort to asserting and showing many
things which are not always themselves common and accepted.
Dewey does this, it seems to me, as convincingly as it can be
done.

The skeptic's argument in one of the more extreme versions runs like this: The world is senseless because, in short,
a man can never know anything beyond the present moment.

He has his present experience of the chair, or table, or whatever the philosopher of skepticism happens to direct his destructive gaze upon. But, it is argued, he has no assurance that the chair was there a moment ago, or that it will be there in the future. The fact that he remembers the chair having been there is insignificant, because memory itself is merely part of the present affections of the man's mind. It is, therefore, something separate and distinct from what it purports to remember.

Likewise, the fact that the man's normal expectations lead him to believe that the chair will remain before him is also insignificant. For this too is merely an image or feeling of the present moment and, hence, does not touch that future which it purports to represent. This present moment is apart and different from the other moments of experience. That is what makes it itself and not something else. Anything in it which purports to be the same as past or future is mere illusion.

In this version, the skeptical doctrine of atomism is applied to human experience. The doctrine can be generalized as an account of all things and processes. The skeptic might argue that all things are composed of separate, distinct, impenetrable particles. He might concede that, by accident or chance, these fundamental atoms affect or penetrate one another. Or he might maintain that they remain forever apart, holding their natures wholly within themselves. In either case, he denies that the fundamental parts of the world regularly enter into and remain within one another.

*Past and Present* Dewey is ready to make the assertions which enable us to avoid these conclusions. He does not just assert them. He shows persuasively that they are founded in experience. He shows that the skeptic is wrong, first, because a man's experience is not simply of the present moment separate from past moments. On the contrary, this present experience literally has the past within it.

Consider, for instance, the business of looking for some object which you have dropped in your front yard. As you

walk around with your eyes on the ground, each act of looking leads to the next and remains active in the next act. That
is fortunate, since if those previous acts did not remain on actively in succeeding acts, these later acts would be without
guidance, allowing you to search the same patch of ground
again and again without realizing that you had already
searched there. In experience, we find from time to time
what Will James called "a compounding of consciousness."[2]

We may go beyond personal experience in the narrow
sense, in order to illustrate the idea. What every practical
man knows is that when he builds a house or makes a loaf
of bread, the things he uses remain on in the house or loaf
of bread. The brick and mortar and lumber and labor do
not simply give rise to the house; they make it. The material,
tools, and labor do not end abruptly and give way to the
house, as a magical spell might create a castle. These means
have *become* their consequence, as anyone can tell by looking
at the house and seeing the clear traces of work, lumber,
bricks, and so on, in the body of the present thing.

"Paints and skill in manipulative arrangement," writes
Dewey, "are means of a picture as end, because the picture is
*their* assemblage and organization . . . Flour, water, yeast are
means of bread because they are ingredients of bread; while
bread is a factor *in* life, not just *to* it. A good political constitution, honest police-system, and competent judiciary, are
means of the prosperous life of the community because they
are integrated portions of that life. Science is an instrumentality of and for art because it is the intelligent factor *in* art.
The trite saying that a hand is not a hand except as an organ
of the living body—except as a working coördinated part of a
balanced system of activities—applies untritely to all things
that are means. The connection of means-consequence is
never one of bare succession in time, such that the element
that is means is past and gone when the end is instituted. An
active process is strung out temporarily, but there is a deposit
at each stage and point entering cumulatively and constitu-

tively into the outcome. A genuine instrumentality *for* is always an organ *of* an end. It confers continued efficacy upon the object in which it is embodied."[3]

Suppose we ask Dewey the familiar question stated by Hume: What is the necessity by which effect follows cause? How can we say that effect *must* follow cause? When we have two "atoms" of experience or nature succeeding one another in time, why may we sometimes say that the latter necessarily follows from the former? Does this alleged necessity amount to anything more than our habit of seeing one follow the other?

To this a Deweyan could reply that the necessity of the relation lies in the fact that the effect is the cause in a new form. What we find is that several causes or means have come together to make a single, unified thing or process. The causes are still present in the effect, but by coming together they have created the effect. The effect includes them, yet is also something they were not—as gin and vermouth make a drink in which one can distinguish both ingredients and yet recognize the further distinctive flavor of a Martini.[4]

So to the skeptic the first part of the reply is that memory is the past, some or all of the past, remaining on actively in the present. The past did not at some moment stop and give way to the present. The past was the means of which the present is the consequence. Between past and present there is continuity.

*Future and Present*  The skeptic impugns not only memory, but also anticipation. Here also the Deweyan reply rests on the principle of means-consequence. Where the means-consequence relation holds, these affections of the present moment which purport to represent the future, literally are the future coming into existence. They are the tendency of the present means to become the future consequence.

"The modern mind," writes Dewey, "has formally abjured belief in natural teleology because it found Greek and medieval teleology juvenile and superstitious. Yet facts have a way of compelling recognition of themselves. There is little scientific writing which does not introduce at some point or other the idea of tendency. The idea of tendency unites in itself exclusion of prior design and inclusion of movement in a particular direction, a direction that may be either furthered or counteracted and frustrated, but which is intrinsic. Direction involves a limiting position, a point or goal of culminating stoppage, as well as an initial starting point. To assert a tendency and to be fore-conscious of a possible terminus of movement are two names of the same facts."[5]

Like Mannheim, Dewey would insist that the facts are never merely "given." There is given fact, that side of experience which is peculiarly its present; and there is another side of experience, the tendency of given fact to become something different. In ordinary thought and behavior, men do not treat these tendencies as something "mentalistic," existing as mere affections of the present moment of experience. They are a real part of the present facts and we overlook any part of them at our peril.

No newspaper man, for instance, can write a dispatch about a certain political situation without some regard for the tendencies of that situation. He may find these tendencies obscure and hard to grasp. But neither he nor his reader doubts that they are really there; and both are concerned to seize upon them so far as possible. In these political tendencies, they discern the men of tomorrow, the policy of next week or next year, growing out of the facts of the present situation.

In all our daily activities we are continually concerned, not only with the given facts, but also with the tendencies of these facts. It is part of the genius of Dewey that he takes words like "tendency," or "means" and "consequence," which sum up so much common experience, and shows how such words illuminate the fundamental problems of philosophy.

The problem which they illuminate here is the relation between the present and future moments of experience. In the means-consequence relation, the means tend to become the consequence. This tendency, working in a man's experience, is his knowledge of what the means will become. His knowledge is not only an affection of the present moment. It is not only a sensory symbol which he manipulates in reflection. It is also the power and tendency of the present to lead to a certain future. Knowledge is power; it makes the future. The truth works; it links the "atoms" of the continuum of experience.

The word "knowledge" may have the wrong emphasis. It may connote a static observer, or static object of contemplation. In explaining Dewey's view, the emphasis should be on the fact that knowledge is "interested." It is active; it is the becoming of something. It is purpose and plan. Knowledge cannot be detached. For then it would no longer be tendency; it would no longer be the becoming of something. It would be that mere affection of the present moment which the skeptic claims is all we have of the future. In the means-consequence relation, a prediction or expectation is also a plan and purpose which leads to, and creates, the future out of the present. Our present expectations and purposes make sense because they are the future coming into existence.

*The Technics of Problem-solving* The idea of the means-consequence relation underlies Dewey's analysis of purposive action. But purposive action, though continuous, is not a smooth and effortless flow of thinking and doing. It is punctuated with problems and strained by tension between organism and environment, mind and nature. Man is involved in the constant flux of things which he must at once conform to and conquer. Yet this flux is the occasion for growth and creativity. Knowledge, growing and developing in the continuum of inquiry, enables man to change himself and the world. This philosophy of flux is also a philosophy of creative intelligence.

When a man finds his purposes balked by the facts, a prob-

lematic situation arises in his experience. This situation does
not present him with a clear definition of a problem. This
situation is confused, indeterminate. Not only the man, but
also the facts are confused, for a problem, like a solution, is
an interaction of experience and nature. The indeterminacy of
the problematic situation lies in the fact that the means
through which the problem-solver expected to achieve a desired consequence will not work. The tentative operations
through which he attempts to solve the problem do not fit together in a unified process.

When involved in a problem, the individual tries to find a
solution by reflecting on similar situations in which he has
been involved in the past, or of which he has learned through
others; as, for instance, a lawyer, when presented with a new
case, may run through his knowledge and records of prece-
dents in order to find an analogue to the given case. Take the
simpler instance of the individual relying on his own previous
experience: In the process of reflection, he searches his memory in an attempt to find an analogue as close as possible to the
given problematic situation. He recalls that in the past, when
certain traits, $a$, $b$, $c$, were present in a situation, they led to
further traits, $d$, $e$, $f$. Reflecting on this past experience, he
identifies the traits, $a$, $b$, $c$, in the present situation and so in-
fers that $d$, $e$, $f$ will follow. In this way he begins to identify
the facts, i.e., discover those operations which will solve the
problem.

We may not think of this process of reflection as being
carried on without contact with the facts. What the problem-solver has already noted about the facts will guide him
in his search for an analogy. And what he may find by way of
analogy will guide him in looking for further traits in the
facts. There is continual interaction between tentative hypotheses and the facts, an interaction which affects both hypotheses and facts. The facts are never described as merely
given. Their description always carries some view concerning
what they will lead to. For these descriptions are not made

for their own sake, but as a means of finding a solution to the problem. And when they identify certain traits in the situation, it is because these traits suggest further traits which may constitute a solution.

This interaction of hypothesis and fact is familiar in government planning. One of the virtues of the independent commission is that, acting under a general grant of power from Congress, it can by alternately testing and revising its plans develop a more detailed and concrete policy than Congress could have originally devised. As the commission tests its plans in action, it becomes far more aware of the real extent and character of the problem than it was when it was originally established. At the same time, it approaches closer to a solution. In governmental, as in individual, problem-solving, it is always tempting to try to proceed by first stating precisely and fully what the problem is, and then going on to find a solution. But it is not easy to separate the two stages of inquiry. For the statement of a problem itself inevitably suggests solutions and these in turn call attention to facts which previously may have been neglected. "Fact-finding" will also be, explicitly or implicitly, "policy-making."

We must also note, as Dewey's theory of continuity would indicate, that any hypothesis which the problem-solver proposes will not be merely a prediction. It will involve some action on his own part. This action may be no more than a verification of the prediction. Yet such verification involves operations by the verifier. Mere observation is impossible. To verify a prediction, the inquirer must at least take up a certain position, observe through certain processes and means, concentrate his attention in a certain way.[6] When objects or events of nature enter experience, they enter into a context of operations.

*Rational Self-realization* In the process of reflection and inquiry, a hypothesis is developed. That is, the first tentative hypothesis, which only partially fitted the facts, is not rejected, but is modified by more inclusive hypotheses until at last one is reached which solves the problem. This final inclusive hypothesis is a judgment. Like the hypotheses from which it developed, it is a plan involving action. Hence, it is not only the plan which solves the problem; it is also the process of solution. The judgment is the whole inclusive process of inquiry and solution, as well as the inclusive plan. In it those operations which initially were in conflict have been integrated with other operations to create a unified set of operations.

On the one hand, a judgment is based on analogy and so is a repetition of past experience. On the other hand, it has sprung, not only from past experience, but also from new experience, and so is different from any past experience. No analogy is ever perfectly exact, neither in science nor in law. It will always integrate some novel traits with the old in a unity which is genuinely creative.

Indeed, to say that the situation was a problem is a way of saying that there was an element of novelty in it which the existing knowledge of the problem-solver did not cover. For even if it was some small problem of daily work which he solved in a moment with some routine operation, still the fact that he was not expecting to perform that familiar operation at that particular time and place, in that particular context, indicates that there was something new and unprecedented in the situation. The future is never precisely like the past.

If the process of inquiry were not creative, the solving of problems would add nothing to our knowledge. We should be merely applying identical rules to identical situations and after the solution of problems would be left with the same body of knowledge as before. In each stage of inquiry analogies and generalizations which have been used to solve problems are themselves added to and developed. In this manner, knowledge, like the common law, grows.

We cannot, therefore, regard our generalizations as "laws," but must regard them as "working hypotheses" which are continually being added to and reinterpreted by further inquiry. Yet within the continuum of intelligent inquiry, prediction is possible. For the solution of new problems does not disprove the old rules, but rather develops them. The old rules remain valid. What they lead us to predict will continue to occur. But process is creative and the future will always hold more than the old rules could foretell. Indeed, human purpose as an integral part of natural process will have a hand in the ceaseless work of creating the future. It will not merely reflect the past, but will help make the future.

In the light of this account, the prospects of human purpose are bright. Of course, purpose must continually struggle; its life-course is a succession of problems. One confusion is clarified only to be succeeded by further confusion. The stable is continually menaced by the precarious. The struggle is hard and forces us constantly to revise our beliefs and habits, but it is not in vain. In its course, knowledge, purpose, and power grow; the old is modified, but maintained in the new. We truly have stability in change.

The change, it must be emphasized, is not merely in means, but also in ends. Inquiry begins when familiar "ends-in-view" are balked by a problem. In the process of inquiry new means are creatively developed; at the same time, the old "ends-in-view" are modified. This follows from the fact that an end or consequence is its means as a unified whole. So in the continuum of inquiry, purposes grow and the personality creatively develops. In this sense, we may think of the process of inquiry as a process of rational self-realization. It is fundamental to Dewey's thought that the principles of intelligent scientific procedure are essentially the same as those of intelligent living.[7]

*Relativity of Truth* Like Mannheim, Dewey would hold that truth is relative in the sense that the "facts" are not merely "given," but are affected by knowledge and purpose. In the interaction of hypothesis and fact, of experience and nature,

both members of the relation are affected. Hypotheses, analogies, rules drawn from past experience, enable the problem-
solver to identify certain facts in the situation. Perception
without such aids is blind. These hypotheses, as a body of
knowledge which a man brings to problem-solving, constitute his perspective or, to use a familiar phrase, his "appercipient mass." And as we have noted, this body of knowledge
is never mere knowledge, but is also purpose and plan which
involve a practical doing on his part. So far our account has
not done much more than arrive at Mannheim's doctrine of
perspective from a different course of analysis.

However, we have noted that the interaction of hypothesis
and fact affects both members. An inquiring mind comes to a
problem with certain purposes, but in its contact with fact
those purposes are modified and enriched. New traits in a
situation may be perceived and that perception will modify
the purposes which were brought to the situation. Thus
creative solutions arise. In the continuum of inquiry, the inquirer's perspective is continually developed. The purposes
and interests which he brings to inquiry guide him in his con-
tacts with the facts. But what he learn about the facts in
turn guides the development of his interests and purposes. If
he is to learn, he must start from what he already knows.
In that sense his approach to the facts is limited and biased
and he is "blind" to many aspects of the facts. But we must
not forget that he can learn and that in the course of learning his initial purposes may be greatly enlarged and deepened.

Perhaps the emphasis on practical doing has obscured this
important point. In spite of Dewey's warning, we incline to
think of purpose as somehow confined to a mind which excludes external nature, and we conclude that since purpose
guides us in our selection of facts, we cannot learn, nor have
our purposes altered by the facts. Yet, as Dewey continually
emphasizes, purpose, mind, experience, are an interaction with
external nature. The object is still what "objects." Facts force
themselves on our attention, whether or not we have seen

anything exactly like them before. So there is this side of the relation which we may think of as mere knowing, mere reception of fact, although we may not separate it from the whole process of interaction. Each side is important. Purposing affects knowing and knowing affects purposing.

One word to apply this conclusion to a notion common in the social sciences. Often the term "social myth" is used in the sense in which we have used the term "perspective." A social myth is held to be a certain way of looking at the facts and acting on them which is common to a group of people. No doubt there are such myths. What should be pointed out is that a myth may not be thought of as a fixed set of principles which cannot be seriously modified and which dictates to a people a line of conduct and thought from which they cannot escape. If we are to follow Dewey's account, we must hold that, like the working hypotheses of science, a social myth is continually in a process of development and enrichment. Social myths are a deposit of past experience, of a people's history, and are as much in flux as the appercipient mass of an individual man.

*Postulate of Continuity*   There is another sense in which we may speak of the relativity of truth. We have considered the relativity of truth to purpose, i.e., the fact that what a man is looking for will have a part in determining what he finds. But Dewey's account introduces another sense of the word. For, according to his account, any particular truth or hypothesis will hold only in a certain context of experience. As knowledge grows, the inquirer will discover that this truth does not hold precisely as it did before and will be obliged to qualify and modify it, though not to reject it utterly.

We should not find it hard to grant part of this view of the relativity of truth. Certainly, it is a fact that our truth, the rules and hypotheses of which our knowledge consists, does not hold forever and without exception. As the world moves, we must continually change the truths on which we operate.

But can we believe that in this course of changing truth the old is always maintained in the new? Do we never reject utterly a truth which we have at one time accepted and acted upon successfully? Can we accept this bright picture of a continuously evolving truth in a process which at bottom is all gain and no loss?

These questions confront us with an assumption which throughout this discussion of Dewey's views has tried to force itself on our attention. It is the assumption of continuity. "The idea of continuity," writes Dewey, "is not self-explanatory. But its meaning excludes complete rupture on one side and mere repetition of identities on the other; it precludes reduction of the 'higher' to the 'lower' just as it precludes complete breaks and gaps. The growth and development of any living organism from seed to maturity illustrates the meaning of continuity."[8] To assume continuity, then, is to assume that there will not be complete breaks with the past, but that there will be growth and development. It is to assume that the means will interact to form the consequence; that the past will be maintained in the future; in short, that in problem-solving the problem will be solved.

No doubt, one must make such as assumption if he is to examine the elements of the means-consequence relation and the continuum of inquiry. But we cannot proceed without questioning this assumption, if we wish honestly to inquire into the status of human purpose. Indeed, the problem of purpose arises precisely because the assumption of continuity does not fit the facts. The fact is that sometimes the means do not become a consequence; sometimes the old is not maintained in the new; sometimes our problems are not solved. Discontinuity is a vivid experience to everyone. Histories, individual, national, international, do not move according to this formula of continuously evolving knowledge and purpose. On many sides, there is death, destruction, loss, pain, frustration.

No one could be more aware of this side of the facts than Dewey. He is not only an acute analyst of continuity; he is also a profound philosopher of pluralism. In the first role, he has stated ideas which have been used fruitfully in many kinds of inquiry, in psychology, sociology, and education. In his second role, where he proposes an answer to what is perhaps the greatest question of philisophy, he is no less noted. "Man," he writes in an eloquent passage, "finds himself living in an aleatory world; his existence involves, to put it baldly, a gamble. The world is a scene of risk; it is uncertain, unstable, uncannily unstable. Its dangers are irregular, inconstant, not to be counted upon as to their times and seasons . . .

"Everything that man achieves is got by actions that may involve him in other and obnoxious consequences in addition to those wanted and enjoyed . . . While unknown consequences flowing from the past dog the present, the future is even more unknown and perilous; the present by that fact is ominous . . . Goods are by grace, not of ourselves . . .

"Our magical safeguard against the uncertain character of the world is to deny the existence of chance, to mumble universal and necessary law, the ubiquity of cause and effect, the uniformity of nature, universal progress, and the inherent rationality of the universe. These magic formulae borrow their potency from conditions that are not magical. Through science we have secured a degree of power of prediction and control . . . But when all is said and done, the fundamentally hazardous character of the world is not seriously modified, much less eliminated."[9]

The postulate of continuity is a convenient assumption. But it remains an assumption in the face of "the miscellaneous and uncoördinated plurals of our actual world."[10] Indeed, if continuity always prevailed, would not experience turn out to be something like that Infinite Self-representative Series which Royce held was the formula of the Absolute?[11]

"Rationality," writes Dewey, "as an abstract conception is precisely the generalized idea of the means-consequence relation as such."[12] If the means-consequence relation always held, the world of experience and nature would be rational. That is the trouble; it often does not hold. The world is irrational. It is a multiverse, not a universe.

*Purpose in a Pluralistic World*   The past is not always in the present. Memory itself bears witness to this fact. How much a man does and learns. How little he remembers. He grows; at least, he changes. Youthful habits and thoughts are pushed out of his behavior. He remembers something of them, but what he remembers hardly does more than remind him of how much he has lost.

The future is not always in the present. The tendencies of fact which we seize on in our purposes are often frustrated. It is not that they are merely deferred for the moment, or rearranged in a larger whole of process. They remain, pressing for existence, but without hope of success. They are the hopes deferred, the "felt necessities" meeting no response, which every man and every society suffers from.

But then have we really escaped from the skeptic? These memories of yours—you call them the past, but you admit that you do not have the whole past in your grasp in order to compare them with it in order to see what they really are. And these purposes of yours—if you grant that they may or may not become the future, then how can you call them existential and say they really are the future coming into existence? Must you not agree with the skeptic that memory and anticipation, truth about the past and the future, are merely affections of the present moment, not really the past and future, but strange distortions and illusions in man's silly head?

In a pluralistic world, planning and purpose can hardly make sense. Suppose we grant that there are periods of con-tinuity in history; that there are times when for "a while" a certain type of society persists and develops, as in the middle period of English feudalism or the early period of American individualism. In such periods there can be planning by in-dividuals and groups, since the supposition is that consequences do not fundamentally disappoint expectations. But sooner or later there will be a break in history; as individual men lose the habits of their youth, so may societies part utterly from institutions of their past.

Some discontinuities men can anticipate; some problems they can solve. But the pluralism of the world promises that sooner or later destruction will come upon us. Our truth is not certain, but contingent, and our only certainty is that it will sometime fail us, we cannot know when. We draw our next breath, *Deo volente*, except that as irrationalists we do not believe in God, but in blind chance.

The test of truth is that it works. And when the truth does work it is a mighty weapon. With this instrument man, working with nature, can plan the world and make his history. But truth which works or does not work, according to chance —in what sense is it truth at any time? For when it does happen to work, how can we say that it is truth which is doing the work? If this instrument may at any moment fail inexplicably, can we believe that it ever has a really important hand in the outcome of events? This trust of ours in human truth—does it spring from an honest view of the facts, or from that ancient enemy, pride?

PART TWO

DOUBT OF RIGHT

## CHAPTER FOUR

# THE RELATIVITY OF MORALS

MANNHEIM AND DEWEY ARE TRYING NOT TO ATTACK, BUT TO defend, intelligence and purpose. This makes more striking the failure of their views to provide that defense. Human purpose is a glorious thing, building cultures, unlocking the secrets of nature—so long as its luck holds. But its luck holds only for "a while." The day of the Lord comes like a thief in the night. If fear of the Lord, an awareness of human frailty, is the beginning of wisdom, then the irrationalists and skeptics must be allowed to have set foot on the path of learning. Surely they are far ahead of the naïve dogmatists who claim that we can plan our future and reduce the world to obedience to our desires.

*Appetite makes Right*   But may this not be precisely the root of our failure to make sense of human purpose: the fact that so far we have approached the problem only from the angle of our "desires"? Purpose does not make sense as a means of gratifying our desires. But may it not be defended as a means of fulfilling the moral law?

So far our inquiry has been very much concerned with consequences. But in ethical thought there is an intimation, which is echoed by our moral feelings, that moral decision should eschew too much concern with consequences. In the course of the debates in the council of Cromwell's Army at a critical time in the Puritan Revolution, a Mr. Wildman aptly expressed this sentiment. As the argument over the question of who was to have the vote waxed hotter and more obscure, he broke in. "Unless I be very much mistaken," he said, "we are very much deviated from the first question. Instead of following the first proposition to inquire what is just, I conceive we look to prophecies, and look to what may be the event, and judge of the justness of a thing by the consequence. I desire we may recall ourselves to the question whether it be right or no."[1]

"Whether it be right or no": this has a rather old-fashioned sound, but it may be a more illuminating approach to the problem of purpose than instrumentalism. The approach has various familiar forms. One is the view that the purposes of the individual should be informed by the dictates of conscience. Another is the notion that the plans of government should express a "natural law" which embodies the fundamental principles of right and wrong. Governments and men should follow these laws and imperatives regardless of consequences. Each must do what is right, let the chips fall where they may. *Fiat justitia, ruat coelum.*

There is, it appears, no way of making the world serve your will. But there is something which your will itself can and should serve. The instrumentalist asks, "What is useful for me?" and finds no answer that is not treacherous and unreliable. The moral man asks, "What am I useful for?" He claims that he finds a law to serve and a duty to perform.

On the one hand is the view that appetite makes right. Word's like "good," "virtuous," "just," it is held, are simply words to denote what someone wants, while words like "bad," "vicious," "unjust" denote what someone does not want. Values are determined by a man's interests, positive or negative. On the other hand is the view that there is a moral law to which man ought to conform his will. He apprehends this law by means of the "moral faculty" or conscience; with greater or less clarity it tells him what he *ought* to do.

This is an old conflict: appetite versus morality; utility versus right. When Protagoras argued that man is the measure of all things, one point he was making was that there is no objective standard of right and wrong to which a man's acts ought to conform. Thomas Hobbes expressed the idea in these words: "Good and Evill, are names that signifie our Appetites, and Aversions; which in different tempers, customes, and doctrines of men, are different."[2] More ambiguous formulae were devised by the English utilitarians. "Pleasure and freedom from pain," wrote John Stuart Mill, for instance, "are the only things desirable as ends."[3] Fundamentally the idea is the same as that expressed more precisely by modern academic philosophers, such as Ralph Barton Perry. "Value," writes Perry, is "the peculiar relation between any interest and its object, or this special character of an object which consists in the fact that interest is taken in it."[4]

In all these writers, the suggestion that there is a Higher Law is repudiated. And at least in this respect John Dewey is at one with them. He shows how the impulses and desires of our nature are transformed by intelligence. But he does not find that there is a standard or law to which those impulses ought to be made to conform.

This view that appetite makes right, however formulated, is both repulsive and dangerous. It is repulsive because it flouts strong human feelings. Possibly people act this way; surely most of them do not think this way. Take the ordinary man of practical affairs who has not been exposed to too much education, the farmer, manual worker, or banker. Try to argue seriously with him that the difference between right and wrong is merely the difference between liking and disliking. The chances are that you will be put down as either communistic or crazy.

All these amoral, utilitarian, pragmatic theories of ethics smell of the lamp. They claim to be naturalistic, but natural men repudiate them. They insist that their principles are founded on human nature, but human nature refuses to accept them. Only sophisticates, theoreticians, men under the power of some self-conscious doctrine, agree that appetite makes right.

Besides, are these theories not dangerous? If appetite alone

makes right, then our cause and our war have no more justification than that of our enemy. The enemy want to make us
work for them; we want to work for ourselves. It is merely
a question of two wants, two natural forces, in conflict, as
when animals fight for food and sex, or stars in their senseless
rounds collide. Fight for your country; be loyal to your flag;
sacrifice for your family, friends, and society—if you feel
like it. Respect the rights of other men; give them their due;
help them when they are in trouble—if you want to. Are
these not dangerous thoughts?

They are at least common thoughts among students of
politics today. Modern government, it is often said, is not an
organ for maintaining rights and duties which belong to men
because of a Higher Law. It is rather an agency for giving
them what they may happen to desire. That is, if groups
and individuals want to use the government as a means to get
what they want, there is no Higher Law, no natural right,
to prevent them. If people want more wages or more profits;
more pensions or more wars or more education, the government is there to be used by them. A raid on the Treasury is
not something to be condemned as selfish and immoral; self-
ishness is merely the word prigs use to indicate the interests
of others. Confiscation; exploitation; these words lose their
moralistic connotation and become words denoting merely
certain practices which in the long run it may be against the
self-interest of a group or a man to indulge in. We are all
after certain consumer's goods and services; the only law
between us is the law set by our own appetites. Such a state
might be called the Consumptive State.

This theory of ethics and politics is repulsive and dangerous. The problem is whether we can find a theory of moral
law which avoids its defects and satisfies the facts. To search
for such a theory will be the object of our inquiry in this
Part. A good deal of progress can be made. In what will be
called the ethics of civilization, we shall find a theory which
overcomes many of the common objections to theories of

ethics. But we shall also find this theory infected with grave defects and shall be forced to conclude that ethics, while it illuminates considerably the problem of purpose, will not solve it, alone and unaided.

*Conscience and Moral Codes*    The trouble with most attempts to state the moral law is that the codes they produce are either too concrete or too abstract. In this chapter we shall see how codes can be too concrete. Call to mind, for instance, some code of conduct which has been taught to young men of a certain class in a certain society. Think of the ideas expressed by fathers in their letters to their sons, or the ordeal of growing up as described by novelists. You immediately see that such a code may be acceptable in some societies, but entirely unsatisfactory in many other societies. The rules and ideas of such a code define fairly concretely what a man ought to know and do, and how he ought to behave toward others. The more concrete the code, the more of a man's conduct it can decide for him; the more of his conduct, that is, which is brought under the rules of what he ought to do.

But it also follows that the more concrete the code, the less applicable it is likely to be in other circumstances. The code of the Southern gentleman in the ante-bellum South may have been satisfactory in that society. It required a certain kind of conduct toward Negroes, women, strangers of one's class, and toward one's elders and superiors, a code of conduct which has often been celebrated in song and story.[5] However, in a society where well-bred women work with their hands and heads, it is no longer necessary or moral to treat them as if they were in crinoline. Where Negroes work for wages and own what they earn, it is no longer moral to treat them as if they were your property. The old code had much to recommend it. But we should hardly say that the man who tried to live strictly by it today would be doing what he ought to do.

The problem is that if a man gets a code which enables him substantially to guide his life, he finds that this code is relative to the time and society in which he lives. Thrift, which is a primary virtue in Vermont or Scotland, is the mark of a prig in the Old South. Occasional fist-fighting, which is more or less obligatory for a man in Frontier America, is cause for ostracism in the settled societies of the East or England. It appears then that these injunctions to save our pennies, or to take no back talk, which have been impressed on our characters by example and precept, are not eternal laws of right and wrong, of honor and dishonor, but the conventions of a little time and place. We feel strongly that there is a Higher Law. But like Antigone we elevate to this status the rules of a local and passing mythology.

When this relativity of moral codes is first pointed out to a man (usually along in his freshman year in college), his belief in conscience and the Higher Law will probably be severely shaken. He finds that other people of another age and place have had a different set of rules as their moral code, a set of rules which is not only different, but perhaps even incompatible with his own. He refuses to think that the conscience of these other people was somehow corrupt, while his own is clear. He concludes, therefore, that conscience itself (if there is such a thing) is unreliable as the voice of the moral law.

The argument can be put in other ways. If conscience is something present in all, or most, men, then we should find some considerable agreement in moral codes. But in fact the more we know about history and anthropology, the more differences we find in men's ideas of right and wrong.

This fact has impressed students in other ages, as well as our own. In the sixteenth century, Montaigne concluded from his haphazard, but penetrating, study of man and society that where men disagree so deeply over the content of the moral law, there can hardly be such a law. "The laws of conscience which we say are born of Nature," he wrote, "are born of custom: as every man holds in inward veneration the opinions and manners received and approved around him, he is unable to let go his hold on them without remorse, or to cling to them without approval." And what was true of morals in general, was true of political ideals in particular. "The nations," he continued, "that have been bred up in liberty and self-rule look upon every other sort of government as abnormal and contrary to nature; those that are accustomed to a monarchy do the like."[6]

It is hardly necessary to point out how often modern students of anthropology and sociology have made similar comparisons and have come to the same conclusion. One of the most impressive statements of this case is William Graham Sumner's *Folkways*, first published in 1906. This work may not take one very far toward a true "science des moeurs," but it is an extraordinary collection of data, tending to show that "the mores can make anything right and prevent condemnation of anything." "The morality of a group at a time," wrote Sumner, "is the sum of the taboos and prescriptions in the folkways by which right conduct is defined. Therefore morals can never be intuitive. They are historical, institutional and empirical."[7] After reading Sumner's account of mores which put the stamp of approval on slavery, abortion, infanticide, the killing of the old, cannibalism, incest, blood revenge, cruel and obscene punishments, public lupanars, sacral harlotry, child sacrifice, and other self-evidently wicked practices, the young man can hardly avoid nodding assent.

A more recent and more sophisticated application of this notion is Ruth Benedict's *Patterns of Culture*. Here an eminent anthropologist describes the weirdly divergent patterns of behavior of several cultures. There are the Indians of Zuñi whose principal interest lay in preparing for and performing ceremonial dances and who held personal power, violence, and leadership in contempt and fear. A less unfamiliar set of ideals is that of the Kwakiutl of the northwest coast of America, whose life centered around great potlatches where rival chiefs put one another to shame by destroying larger and larger quantities of their own goods. Among the natives of Dobu, an island off the coast of New Guinea, treachery and ill will are virtues, and theft and adultery are the objects of the valued charms of the valued men of the community.

Like Montaigne and Sumner, Miss Benedict takes as one of her principal themes the power of custom over the character of the individual and the great differences between cultures. There are a vast number of ways that men can act and different cultures have "chosen" different ways. "The cultural pattern of any civilization," she writes, "makes use of a certain segment of the great arc of potential human purposes and motivations, just as we have seen . . . that any culture makes use of certain selected material techniques or cultural traits. The great arc along which all the possible human behaviors are distributed is far too immense and too full of contradictions for any one culture to utilize even any considerable portion of it."[8]

The great arc of human possibility: a fascinating figure of speech, and behind it lies a metaphysical idea.

*Natural Law*  When moral codes are compared, one effect is likely to be a shaking of a man's trust in the sanction of the Higher Law, his trust in conscience. This moral faculty, this sense which, without explaining why, tells him categorically that he *ought* to behave in a certain way—why should he take it seriously? This still, small voice merely echoes the accents of some hidden master, of habit, custom, education, sniggering public opinion.

Another effect is to suggest that any moral code, which is concrete enough to enable a man to guide his life, must be relative to a certain society. For one thing, the specific acts required by this act involve a certain kind of environment, social and natural. When this environment changes, the old acts lose their character and no longer make sense. The only things Don Quixote *could* tilt at were windmills and sheep.

Moreover, the morality of the acts themselves is altered when the environment changes. In the new society, the old morality sometimes becomes positively immoral.

The history of the doctrine of natural law can be used to illustrate this conclusion. How precisely to use the term and what connection to give it with ethics are matters which we need not decide now. Here it is enough to grant that the terms "natural law" and "law of nature" have often been taken to indicate a set of rules which government ought to follow, ultimately because of some moral sanction.[9]

During the closing years of the nineteenth century, the United States Supreme Court began to elaborate what may be called a system of natural law. This term was not commonly used, but the meaning was the same when the court declared that there were certain fairly specific practices which were protected by the Constitution and sanctioned morally by a Higher Law.[10] The Constitution did not define in terms what these practices were. Rather the Court deduced that they were protected from the general phrases of the Constitution, especially the prohibitions which state that no person shall be deprived of "life, liberty or property, without due process of law." Precisely what is meant by these words is not clear at first glance, and the court undertook the task of stating in particular what rights were intended.

An instance of the way the court applied itself to this task is provided by the concurring opinion of Mr. Justice Bradley in the second Slaughterhouse case of 1884. "The right to follow any of the common occupations of life," he wrote there, "is an inalienable right; it was formulated as such under the phrase 'pursuit of happiness' in the Declaration of Independence which commenced with the fundamental proposition that 'all men are created equal, that they are endowed by their Creator with certain inalienable rights; that among these are life, liberty and the *pursuit of happiness.*' This right is a large ingredient in the civil liberty of the citizen. To deny it to all but a few favored individuals by investing the latter with a monopoly, is to invade one of the fundamental privileges of the citizen, contrary not only to common right, but, as I think, to the express words of the Constitution."[11]

The "express words" to which the justice referred were the vague phrases of the first section of the Fourteenth Amendment, among them the due process clause with its protection of "liberty." But it is not hard to see how he finds a specific rule in these vague phrases. He takes the word "liberty" in the due process clause and holds that it includes "the right to follow any of the common occupations of life," i.e., the customary ways of making a living in America in the latter part of the nineteenth century. It follows that the attempt of a legislature to modify these customs must infringe upon constitutional liberty and also "common right," or morality.

Under various headings, the court in later years proceeded to declare what practices were protected by the due process clause. When it was a question of rate regulation, the court held that the notion of "reasonableness" governed its particular decisions. Where the state legislature sought to regulate prices, the court tried to confine regulation to certain businesses which it found were "affected with a public interest." Laws touching wages and hours were held invalid when they infringed "liberty of contract." These terms in themselves were as ambiguous as the phrases of the due process clause. As has often been pointed out, the content which the court gave them reflected in general the business customs of American society in the last quarter of the nineteenth century.[12]

This system of natural law as developed by the courts was hardly free of inconsistencies. But the criticism which should be emphasized here is not that it lacked concreteness, but that it was so concrete as to be satisfactory only in the setting of American society between the Civil War and World War I. The perfectionist will no doubt object that this kind of society and the system of rights sustaining it were at no time satisfactory. However, it must be recalled that the doctrine of laisser-faire was still the faith of many social reformers in the Anglo-Saxon world after the Civil War,[13] and that this faith was not then misplaced. Even in the period 1900-1914, price competition still flourished in the American economy; employment grew considerably; productivity rose; and the gains it represented were largely passed on to the consumer.[14] Judged by results, the system was still working. But after World War I, and especially after the onset of the Great Depression, the old system of rights, which the court persisted in enforcing, no longer had the consequences which had originally given it meaning.

For instance, there may have been no great need to permit state legislatures to fix minimum wages in the late eighteen-eighties. It may have been satisfactory then to guarantee "liberty of contract" as a natural right. But by 1936 the facts of our society had been profoundly altered. The kind of employment previously provided by a constantly expanding frontier was gone, and competition between employers had greatly declined. Even where jobs were being created, the size of businesses made the individual employee a weaker bargainer than he had been two or three generations before.

These and other circumstances made some kind of wage regulation desirable. Yet in 1936 the Supreme Court forbade state legislatures to regulate wages and upheld as a constitutional right the "liberty" of employer and employee to bargain about wages without interference from government.[15] In effect, the court was enforcing as a natural right a business custom which had been satisfactory only in the social context of another age. The old morality had become positively immoral.

In the present chapter, we have seen that what people regard as good or satisfactory has varied immensely from society to society. We have also seen that, as society evolves, it is necessary that moral and legal codes should change in order to remain satisfactory. If the good or the satisfactory is to be achieved, there must be continual novelty in our moral codes, just as, regardless of our wishes, there invariably is novelty in the natural world.

## CHAPTER FIVE

# THE ETHICS OF COMMUNITY

WHAT MEN REGARD AS RIGHT AND WRONG VARIES GREATLY from one society to another. The moral sense, or conscience, of a man seems to be relative to the society or age in which he lives. Indeed, the moral sense must be relative; that is, it must change as the context of society changes. For systems of law and morals tend to lose their meanings as society changes. Only if the moral sense keeps pace with society, can we expect to have a code which is satisfactory.

But here we have introduced a further conception. We seem to have some standard or principle in mind by which we judge particular moral codes satisfactory or unsatisfactory. It seems, then, that the moral sense is not limited to the rules of a particular code, but includes more general ideas. It seems that while specific systems of morals are transient and relative, there are certain general principles which are at least more constant and less relative. Perhaps this, rather than specific moral codes, is the direction in which to look for the formulation of the Higher Law, and the true sense of conscience.

*Fundamental Moral Maxims* If we consider the case of wage regulation again, a rationalization in terms of more general moral principles might be worked out on these lines: We feel that a man doing useful work ought to receive a wage which enables him to keep his mental and physical health. We find that in the 1880's laisser-faire in general provided this "living wage," but that fifty years later, it was necessary for government to step in in order to ensure similar consequences. The moral principle has remained the same; the particular application has changed. We might go on to enumerate other such principles. Our feelings about political and civil freedom could be generalized. In such general ideas we could find similarities which link Americans of the age of big business, great cities, and trade unions with the Americans of Jefferson's day. Such a set of general principles is an elusive thing, hard to put into words. Yet we should admit that there is an American Spirit, or way of life, which we share with past generations from which we differ greatly in concrete institutions and particular social habits.

But it is also evident that such a code is open to the objection which was raised against the more specific codes. It also is relative to a time and place, although, because of its greater generality, to a wider time and place. There are, it must be conceded, many societies for which the American way of life is not suitable. There are many peoples to whom the practices which Americans have regarded as duties for a hundred and fifty years would appear as outlandish as the code of the Southern gentleman appeared to the Yankee. If we seek a deep contrast, we can get it by comparing some of our institutions, such as the family, with those of the Near East or the Orient. Hardly less sharp contrasts appear when we look at some of the customs of other Western nations, such as the British.

Then is there not some general notion which is the common core of morality for nearly all peoples and all ages? At least all, or nearly all, have this much in common: they do have a system of morality. Even the primitive peoples whose particular standards are so different from ours, in some measure accept, and feel obliged by, these standards. Different societies have different laws, but at least they are similar in that each has *a* law. In some measure, each has a code which enables its members to live and work together in harmony and coöperation.

To live together in harmony and coöperation: Is this the

ideal which our moral feelings try to realize and which particular moral codes, with greater or less success, try to formulate? There is nothing startling in the suggestion. "For all the law," one authority has said, "is fulfilled in one word, in this: Thou shalt love thy neighbor as thy self." To love your neighbor as yourself is to make his interest your interest and to direct your work as much toward accomplishing his task as toward accomplishing your own. It is to live with him in a harmony which does not consist merely in a lack of friction, but rather in the positive pursuit of a common end. When several men love one another, they are pursuing a common purpose; they are living in community with one another. Let us see how far the notion of community can take us toward an answer to the problem of purpose.

*Kant on Community* Immanuel Kant was a philosopher of community. But the name which he used to refer to the leading conception of his ethics was not "community," but "reason." Kant started from what he regarded as a fact, namely, that a man does have a conscience, a sense of right and wrong. According to Kant, the command of this sense of right, the categorical imperative, is that man should be rational. "The basis of obligation," he wrote, "must not be sought in the nature of man, or in the circumstances in the world in which he is placed, but *a priori* simply in the conceptions of pure reason."[1]

This attempt to find in reason the idea which should fix the fundamental ideal of man may seem curious to us today. We are used to thinking of "the function of reason" as merely the task of showing given desires how to attain their ends. We find it hard to see how reason itself can fix an end for us. We think of the power of reason as something like the ability to think straight, make inferences, solve problems. We think of the "information" which the principle of reason contains as certain fundamental propositions of logic, such as the principles of identity, contradiction, and excluded middle.

We find it hard to see how the power which operates according to these bare principles can provide us with an ideal.

Yet this attempt to root morality in rationality, to say that conscience speaks with the voice of reason, is common in the history of thought. For instance, in the political debates of Englishmen in the seventeenth century, when a man spoke of "reason" he was as likely to mean the power to tell right from wrong as the power to think straight.[2] When one reads Blackstone, he gets the idea that this archaic and confused mass of rights enforced by the common law in the eighteenth century was commanded or revealed by reason. Similarly, our own Supreme Court has often used the term "reasonable" as a synonym for fair or just. The commonest defect of such attempts is that "reasonable" turns out to mean little more than "conventional"; as, for instance, when a court finds that 6 per cent is a reasonable return on a utilities investment.

Still, it is not hard to see why men should be anxious to identify the principles of reason and right. Reason is supposed to reveal to us certain abstract, but necessary, truths about fact. Can it be shown that the dictates of conscience express these same fundamental truths, commanding us to apply them to our intentions toward one another? If so, it appears that laws which are unconditionally true of fact are felt by men as unconditional moral imperatives on their purposes and intentions. One advantage of this conclusion is that it makes it easier for us to understand the specific mandates of conscience, since we now know the principles from which they proceed. There is another reason why men are attracted to this conclusion, but it is harder to put into words: To show that the principles of morality proceed from reason somehow adds to the plausibility of morality itself. Reason stands for the immutable and certain. If morality is rational, it shares in this aura of certainty.

But before we grant that reason informs our sense of right, this question clamors for an answer: What are those necessary truths which reason reveals to us? For some thinkers, the dogmatic rationalists, reason revealed a set of propositions which constituted a body of more or less general laws of nature. But to Kant such a view was not acceptable; the self-evident truths which had commonly formed the base for systems of natural law did not seem self-evident to him.

When in the *Critique of Pure Reason* he was investigating the process of knowing, he found that the mind, in perceiving a succession of events, apprehends them in a certain unity. It may apprehend them in the unity of cause and effect, or in the unity of substance and attribute, or other of the twelve categories of understanding which Kant held to be necessary modes of thought. In short, Kant had a theory of perspective in which he set out the way by which the mind will invariably approach and understand the facts. We are not interested in the particulars of his theory, but only in his insistence that the mind will impose a unity on separate phenomena. For it is in this "originally synthetical unity of apperception" that we find the heart of his notion of reason.

In his writings on ethics, Kant turns from considering the activity of reason in the apprehension of fact to its activity in relation to human conduct; from its activity in knowing to its activity in purposing. Here reason appears as a faculty or principle which attempts to impose unity on the conduct of the individual in relation to himself and to other men. Here the dictates of reason do not have that force or necessity which makes them hold invariably in the apprehension of fact. Their necessity is a moral necessity. The dictates of the categorical imperative indicate what unconditionally ought to be, even though in fact these dictates may never be followed.

The best known of his formulations of the imperative runs as follows: "Act only on that maxim whereby thou canst at the same time will that it should become a universal law."[3] It is the dictate that a man ought to impose unity or law upon his own successive acts and upon his acts in relation to other men.

This famous sentence has had various interpretations. As

developed by Kant, it does not seem to go beyond the principles of identity and contradiction. "If *A*, then *A*." "If *A*, then not *not-A*": these are hardly illuminating sentences. But if we apply them to the relations of men's purposes, we get the nub of the idea of community. First of all, each individual man should be governed in his various acts by a single law or purpose; between these acts, there should be identity not contradiction. Secondly, between the acts and purposes of different men, there should also be identity and not contradiction; they should express a single purpose, a single will.

*Common Purpose as Identical Purpose*   What is meant by saying that between the acts of each man and of all men there should be identity? Does this mean that a man must continually do the same thing? And that the members of a group must follow identical lines of conduct? That is absurd, and even if it could in some degree be done, it would hardly contribute to the unity and harmony of a society.

Yet this absurd interpretation of Kant's formula is worth pausing over for a moment. For it calls to mind ideas which are important in our feelings about ethics. As applied to the individual, this interpretation suggests that, while a man's acts will necessarily differ, yet each should spring from the same set of fundamental beliefs and convictions. It suggests that the good man will not be one person at one time and another at another time, but will express the same character in all his various acts. In short, that an element of goodness in a man is his integrity, or continuity, of character. And as we develop our theory of ethics we shall modify, but not reject, this sentiment.

Similarly, when applied to a group, this interpretation of Kant's formula brings to mind the fact that a community cannot exist unless there is some identity, some homogeneity, in the behavior of its various members. For instance, when critics consider the relations of men in great cities where groups are separated from one another by sharp cleavages in class, occupation, and social background, they often comment that in such situations there cannot be a true community. And they may go on to compare urban societies with small towns or rural groups where certain similarities of occupation and behavior make community possible. Again, when writers describe the traits of "national character" or the elements of the "fundamental unity" of a country, they often bring to light certain important identities of behavior between the members of a nation-state. As we shall see, these views do get at certain significant facts about community. Some homogeneity of conduct is no doubt necessary in order that the members of a community may have that common understanding which is fundamental to common purpose.

But, in spite of these qualifications, we cannot interpret common purpose to mean identical purpose. The unity of a society, no more than the unity of an individual's conduct, cannot reside in the identities of its elements. For if these elements are working together, it is because there are differences between them which make them complementary. These differences require one another for their own completion. There is unity because one man's way of living requires that other men shall live and work in their own ways, in order that he himself may carry on with his own line of conduct. We shall arrive at a more acceptable theory of community and at another interpretation of Kant, if we consider the thought of Jean Jacques Rousseau.

*Rousseau on Community*   Like Kant, upon whom he had a profound influence, Rousseau sought to root the principles of morality and justice in some notion of pure reason, or "the mere conception of law," to use a phrase of Kant's. According to Rousseau, there was no particular set of rules, no fundamental law, which ought to govern every society; the only law binding on all societies and all men was that within any group there should be *a* law, a system of law. Rousseau develops this point in the opening chapters of his

*Social Contract.* The mark of right between men, one gathers from his argument, is that a law is established between them. He is helped in making this equivalence of "right" and "law" by the double meaning of the French word, *droit.* There can be no "right" of slavery, because the slave-master has un-limited power over his slave, while a right is a particular, de-fined, and, therefore, limited power over something or some-one. The argument is even more striking if we start from the other meaning of the word, *droit:* There can be no "law" of slavery, because the master-slave relation is one in which there is no law defining the relationship and fixing a line of conduct to which both parties must conform.

Similarly, argues Rousseau, there cannot be a contract which gives rise to the "right" of slavery, because a contract has terms and stipulations, binding both parties to something definite in the way of conduct. But slavery is precisely that social relation in which one man has power over another man and no stipulations binding both parties are respected.

Rousseau is not trying to prove that men have a sense of right or justice. Like Kant, he assumes that they have such a sense, and in his argument he is trying to elucidate the dictates of that sense. The substance of his argument is that if these dictates are to be met, men must follow certain laws or rules which define their rights and duties and which all parties un-derstand and accept. The master-slave relation is the antithesis of this ideal condition and so, by contrast, helps define the ideal.

He describes the ideal by means of the fiction of a social contract. That contract is made by each man with all other men in the group. Its formula runs as follows: "Each of us puts his person and all his power in common under the su-preme direction of the general will, and, as a body, we re-ceive each member as an indivisible part of the whole."[4] As a result of this contract, the group becomes a community. The general will lays down those laws, or common purposes, which are binding on all and which are understood and accepted by all. Yet, it may be said in passing, the general will is not identical with these laws or purposes. Rather, it is like Kant's faculty of pure reason which enables the mind to grasp the particular categories of the understanding, but which is not identical with those categories.

*Common Understanding* In Rousseau's formula of the social contract, we may discern the two principal elements of community: first, common understanding, and second, unconditional loyalty.

The notion that every man, or any man, actually did make such a contract is a fiction, and, of course, Rousseau knew it. But it is not a useless fiction, for it points up the fact that common purpose rests upon knowledge and understanding, upon commonly shared meanings and conceptions, not mere gregariousness. This same element is central to contract. When a man agrees to do something in return for something else, he makes a promise. This promise, if he is sincere, is a purpose, a plan, a conception of his future line of conduct. He knows what he is doing; and what brings him to do it is this "mere" knowledge, this "mere" purpose, of his.

Under Rousseau's contract, different roles may be assigned to different persons and groups within the community. But each understands what his role is and what the role of the others is and how these complementary functions are joined in the unified pattern of social conduct. The common purpose expressed by the general will is an idea present in the minds of all members. The contract gives rise to this idea and it is this idea which guides the members of society in their relations with one another.

Without trying to attribute our views to Rousseau, we may examine further this first element of community. Where there is common understanding between two or more people, it means that each knows what the other is doing. And to know what another person is doing is to know how to do what he is doing. For knowledge which is knowledge of *what* an operation is, without being knowledge of *how* to perform that operation, is hardly to be considered knowledge.

Dewey makes a relevant point in distinguishing communication from animal signaling. Animal signals do not involve meaning or purpose. A baby's scream, for instance, attracts the attention of the adult and evokes a response useful to the infant, althought the cry itself is an organic overflow having no intent. But in communication, the response of each participant is from the standpoint of the other.

For instance, where one of two persons points to an object, the second person responds, not to the mere act of pointing, but to the meaning which he believes the other attaches to this motion and which he also understands. Hence, in his response, for example, he does not grasp the pointed finger, but rather picks up the object and brings it to the other. He perceives the object as it may function in the experience of the other, instead of just ego-centrically. "Something," writes Dewey, "is literally made common in at least two different centres of behavior. To understand is to anticipate together; it is to make a cross-reference which, when acted upon, brings about a partaking in a common, inclusive undertaking."[5]

The function of a common "know-how," shared by the members of a coöperating group, can readily be illustrated. To take an example from military experience: when you are training the members of a gun-crew to handle an artillery piece, you will probably teach each member how to perform the tasks of the others. There are various sound reasons for this—to relieve the monotony, to discover who can do each job best, and so on. But there is another reason which becomes evident in practice. Such a common "know-how" makes a far more efficient crew. Each now understands how the others are performing their shares of the common work and can, therefore, more intelligently guide his own work and integrate it with that of the others.

To insist upon common understanding as an element of community is to set limits on the use of the term which are not always recognized. Not every group in which there is harmonious action is a community. For that harmony may proceed from other sources than common understanding. It may proceed from the commands of a leader or boss who performs the task of coördination which in a community is performed by a commonly understood purpose. Or that harmony may proceed from a set of habits and customs which guide the members of the group in a coördinated process without their understanding that process as a whole. In such a group the use of speech, writing, and other signs by the members in relation to one another is more in the nature of animal signaling than communication. To tell whether or not a group is a community, the social scientist cannot rest with merely observing the actions of its members; he must also infer from those actions certain conclusions about their purposes and states of mind. The task of the social scientist requires not only the qualities of the natural scientist, but also the imagination and sympathy of the artist.

Is it not a fact that many of the groups in which we find a certain harmony and unity are communities in only a very partial sense? Much of the coördination of our society and its constituent groups springs not from common purposes, but from blind habituation and command.

How far this is the case is not our problem here. But clearly in many relationships there are matters which are not, and perhaps cannot be, subject to communication and common understanding. To some extent, one man can recreate for himself the experience of others from similar elements in his own experience. One function of artists, poets, novelists, and other men of superior imagination is to help him in this task, and to portray the many vital elements of experience which are common to most men. Yet even for a powerful imagination the lines of communication must soon grow thin and weak. Childbirth, war, sex, hard manual labor—how can matters of this kind be communicated to those who do not know something of them at first hand? If on such matters words fail, it is because a common understanding based on common experience is lacking. Words rest on that body of knowledge or understanding which constitutes the perspective of a man or group. Where perspectives are fundamentally divided, words will hardly build a bridge between them.

The term community may be applied to a group only with great caution. Before the term can be applied, a difficult question of fact must be determined: How many persons in the group share in a common purpose and how many of their relationships are governed by that purpose? In considering any particular case, recall Rousseau's formula: "Each of us puts his person and all his power in common under the supreme direction of the general will, and, as a body, we receive each member as an indivisible part of the whole." Does this trade union or interest group or nation state which you are considering, absorb the "whole person" of its members? Does the purpose of the group include all the fundamental purposes of its members? Does each member understand the fundamental purposes of each of the other members?

*Unconditional Loyalty*  Along with common understanding, we may discern a second element in Rousseau's formula of community. Without conflict with his thought, we could say that there may be groups which are governed by common purposes, but which are not true communities. Such a group would be one in which the members agree to perform some common work, in order to get some particular advantage for themselves; as, for instance, men often do in their business undertakings. Such a group lacks the second element in Rousseau's formula, the element of unconditional loyalty.

Rousseau's formula emphasizes that in the social contract each member of the group puts his person and all his power under the direction of the common purpose. He does not condition his acceptance of the common purpose on the return of some advantage from the community, although he may receive such advantages. He does not say, "If the community continues to provide me with these certain things, then I will continue to abide by its purpose." He is attached to the community for its own sake. In the dictates of the common purpose, he finds an imperative with unconditional moral necessity. To use the terms made familiar by R. M. MacIver, each member is attached to the common purpose as his primary, rather than as a secondary, common purpose.[6]

This second element of community may be spoken of as the "sociality of the self." In this use the term refers to the fact that a man may see his own immediate behavior as an inseparable part of a process in which other men are also making and doing things. His own fundamental purposes integrally involve an understanding of the coöperative activities of his fellows. He can no more conceive of his purposes in isolation from theirs than he can imagine his stomach digesting without food, or his lungs breathing without air. He loves these neighbors as himself, because his "self" involves the "selves" of his neighbors.

Nowadays it is hardly startling to assert that human nature is social. Yet it has not been many years since the hypothesis was thought new and rather shocking. For instance, when F. H. Bradley published his *Ethical Studies* in 1876, it took some brass (which he did not lack) to assert that the individual is inseparably a part of his society; that the "essence of human nature involves identity with others."[7] The reigning view of human nature was not far from the belief that individuality "lies in a sort of inner self, to be cherished by enclosing it, as it were, in an impervious globe."[8]

We today are only too aware of the influence of society on the purposes of the individual. Our anthropologists and sociologists have richly documented that thesis. Mannheim, as we have noted, insists that the perspective of the individual is social; that it springs from his action, not as a solitary being, but as a member of a group. And Dewey has been among the foremost in pointing out the profound effect of society on the habits and behavior of the individual.[9]

Of course, merely to be influenced by others in your purposes does not ensure your unconditional loyalty to a common purpose shared with them. Such influence may attach you to a group through blind habituation, rather than common understanding. Yet the line between the two types of attachment is not always easy to draw and much of what seems to be blind, or irrational, attachment on closer examination may be found to rest on an underlying common understanding.

*Community and Moral Codes*   Such are the two principal elements in the theory of community. In what sense can this formula be said to be derived from the notion of reason? Or rather, what is the meaning of reason expressed in this formula?

In the first place, taking reason as the notion of unity, this formula is rationalist in that the common purpose of a true community imposes a unity upon the social group. Each act of each individual is governed and directed by this purpose. In the second place, taking reason as the power of ideas, this formula is rationalist in that it emphasizes human purposiveness; that is, the ability of mind to impose a unity on events through purposes which govern present and future stages of experience. The promises and plans of men are not held to be blind affections of the present moment, but to be real tendencies which will lead to the conduct which they foreshadow. According to this theory, there can be a real togetherness of events; and ideas are the means by which that unity is achieved and the assurance that it will be achieved.

But we must note immediately that these last assertions go farther than the inquiry of the first part of this book will permit. We must modify them, concluding that the theory of community holds that we ought to frame our purposes *as if* ideas were not illusions and *as if* there could be a real togetherness of events. That is not an un-Kantian conclusion.

In whatever way we refer to this theory—as the Rule of Reason, the Law of Love, or the theory of Community—do we find in it the fundamental idea of morality and the true sense of conscience? Is this the germinal thought which particular transcient moral codes or systems of natural law try to express?

One function of a moral code may be to call attention to an underlying common purpose. Nearly every man has some primary common purposes which he shares with some other men. But normally these purposes, these fundamental sympathies, drop out of his immediate attention. And "normally" means when the plan of coöperation is working smoothly. For then his principal responsibility is to do with the utmost efficiency the immediate task assigned to him by the plan.

But suppose that there arises a threat to the common work, though not immediately to him. The dictates of his moral code will tell him that it is his duty to do something to help his fellows. At first, he may resist these dictates. He may distrust the power which they seem to have over him. If he is an educated man, he may take them to be merely "irrational drives" or "sentiments" or reflexes conditioned to release upon the waving of flags or the ringing of bells, as it is with the poor rats in the psychologist's laboratory. But when he examines the feelings which underlie these dictates, he finds that these feelings, instead of being foreign to his ordinary interests, are a deeper part of them; that his own "self" deeply involves the "selves" of his fellows.

Suppose he tries to forget these feelings and to go back to his habitual round of activities. He will discover a strange thing. These daily habits look the same; yet they have lost their savor. If he is to retain what made them attractive, he must modify them in accordance with his conscience, those deeper feelings of common purpose which attach him to his fellows. It is in some such sense, it seems to me, that conscience has been referred to as "the call of the whole to the part."[10]

A similar analysis is sometimes used to explain the grounds of political obligation. It is said that sometimes when a government coerces, or threatens to coerce, certain people, it is expressing a common purpose which these people have forgotten or overlooked. It is said that here the command of government expresses the "real" will of these people as against their "actual" will, which is their desire of the moment.[11]

If this argument is taken to mean that all commands of all governments are so justified, then it is absurd and not a little wicked. But if it is used as a tool of analysis, it is suggestive and often true to the facts. It is a fact that sometimes the laws must have sanctions because otherwise people, by disobeying them, would fail to do what they fundamentally want to do. Whether this is so is a matter, not of theory, but of fact, and only careful investigation of the facts can prove or disprove it.

A moral code, we may say, often gives a men in abbreviated form a conception of the fundamental relations of the community of which he is a member. In such a case, the moral code presents to a man the typical interests, customs, and institutions of his community. Some practices are characteristic of many codes and many communities. Hence, the familiar moral maxims of folklore and philosophy. But maxims are usually inadequate symbols of the complex relationships of community. We are often better reminded of these things by the lives of our heroes, or by folk stories, or by the history of the community itself. And behind these moral maxims and emotional symbols we may find the idea of reason.

CHAPTER SIX

# THE ETHICS OF
# CIVILIZATION

COMMUNITY IS SOMETIMES A FACT, ALTHOUGH POSSIBLY AN
obscure fact. But we are looking for an imperative. If we
were to state the theory as an imperative, we should try to
express the idea that all wills ought to share a common purpose.
We should say that the ideal would be a condition where all
men coöperated in the service of a commonly understood and
accepted purpose and that, therefore, every man's duty here
and now is to do what he can to create such a condition.
Our fundamental law of purpose would be to work for a
universal purpose. To such a law our purposes should conform, regardless of the apparent irrationality of events and
consequences.

*Community too Abstract*  Our moral feelings will not reject such an imparative, yet in it they will still be far from
complete expression. For granting that we ought to aim at a
universal purpose, we must still ask, What ought to be the
content of that universal purpose? We extend our relations
by establishing particular common purposes which involve
particular lines of conduct. Is it entirely indifferent to moral
theory what particular purposes and processes we establish?

To the theory of community, at any rate, this is a matter
of indifference, for all that its imperative requires is that there
should be a common purpose, a harmony of willing. It cannot
guide us in deciding what the content of a common purpose ought to be. A common purpose may establish a community of men hunting, or playing cards; a pastoral or a
medieval or an industrial community. That it have the charac-

teristics of community is all that the imperative requires. For this reason, the theory of community has often been accused of formalism. The dictates of moral codes, we observed, were "too concrete." The imperative of community proves to be "too abstract."

The defect in the theory of community appears if we try to use its imperative to solve some particular problem. Suppose two groups, such as farmers and workers, come into conflict. The imperative puts no obligation upon these groups to try to preserve the interests and skills which they have already developed. It puts all emphasis on harmony and no emphasis on what is harmonized. So in the light of the imperative, it is quite acceptable to suggest as a solution that the two groups give up their respective occupations and return to a simpler state of society in which the interests giving rise to the conflict do not exist and in which a unifying common purpose can more easily be found. Such a fantastic proposal will strike us as being neither moral nor practical. Still, we have heard people suggest that the way to escape from the conflicts of industrial society is to "go back to the land" and to the allegedly more harmonious society of our forefathers.[1]

The defect of formalism is common in Kantian theories of ethics. For instance, it appears in the theory of "just law" developed by a prominent German Kantian, Rudolf Stammler, professor of law in the University of Berlin two generations ago. In his *Theory of Justice*,[2] Stammler states the conception of just law, a conception which is to be used both as a guide in legislation and in the interpretation of the civil code. As he states this conception, it is substantially the notion of community or common willing.

According to Stammler, when there is a conflict between men, the task of just law is to settle the conflict according to its principles. Thereupon the task of ethics is to teach men to accept the settlements of just law. Just law lays down an external line of conduct for the parties to the conflict; ethics teaches them to will that line of conduct.

But now the difficulty appears. If this is the task of ethics; if the imperative is that one ought to will the settlement of just law, then we must ask what limits there are upon the settlement which just law may make. May it not, indeed, make any settlement whatsoever, so long as the duties it assigns to each party are in natural fact compatible? For in the end the idea of just law is that there should be common willing. So if men are obliged to will the settlement of just law, then it may make any settlement it pleases, since in any case there will be common willing. The trouble is that the standard of just law has no content apart from the common willing which is to succeed its settlement.

The purposes of individual men are in themselves morally important. That a child should grow to adulthood; that a man should build an organization or a business; that a student should make his discoveries: that such things should be done is important, not merely that they should be done in a community.[3]

When considering Dewey's analysis of the continuum of inquiry, we sketched the general manner in which purpose develops intelligently and creatively. Such development occurs in a social context. But for the sake of analysis we may abstract from that context. By so doing we can see more clearly that the development of the personality has a value even when its social relations are not considered. We are under obligation to help one another. But helping others is not the only good open to us. Success in learning and practicing a trade, profession, or science; the adventure of exploring and experimenting in the various worlds of society and nature— this sort of enrichment of the personality is also a good. Community touches a vital spot in ethical theory. But we must not let the forest lead us to overlook the trees. Morality involves individual as well as social values.

To allow for the individual aspect of morality we need not reject the theory of community. We should, rather, interpret it as a mode of procedure in dealing with the purposes of individual men. Reason in itself cannot utter a shining book of laws which tell each man just what he is to make of himself. But it does mark out a way to treat purposes which are struggling for expression. Reason suggests how the purposes of men by being brought into community may themselves be enriched and developed. An ethics founded on this approach is different from the ethics of community, although it includes that ethics. To set it off, let us give it the name "ethics of civilization." In our ordinary use of the term civilization we recognize two senses which correspond to the dual emphasis of this ethics. We understand the advance of civilization to include greater understanding and coöperation among men, as well as an increase in the skill, power, insight of individuals.

*The Principle of Reconciliation*   Let us consider how reason can be understood as a mode of procedure where purposes are in conflict or in isolation. We take as the imperative of reason the obligation to try to bring purposes into community without impairing or injuring them. Our task is the task of reconciliation.

Where the purposes of men are in conflict or in isolation, our task is to look for that creative hypothesis which will reconcile them in a unified social process. Such a hypothesis, if successful, will not impair the given purposes, but will add to and adjust them. It will constitute a common purpose which includes and goes beyond the given purposes and which results in a harmony of behavior between the originally conflicting or isolated men or groups. In short, we shall attempt to apply the technics of problem-solving.

There are other ways, it must be noted, of applying the technics of problem-solving to problems of conflicting or isolated purposes. For example, when a conflict arises, one group sometimes tries to solve the problem by treating the other group as a part of mere nature. It pays no attention to the claims and purposes of the other group, except so far as they provide clues to how it can subdue the other to its will. The solution will be to kill off the members of the other group; to threaten them until they submit; or so to bamboozle them with propaganda that they forget what they were trying to do and accept the place allotted them by the conquerors.

No doubt such operations, where successful, solve the conflict of fact. Like the operations of Goebbels, Goering, and Hitler they may display intelligence of a high order. But an essential of the ethics of civilization is that it is concerned not only with the conflict of mere fact. It is also concerned with the conflict of purpose. Its imperative directs that we solve the problems of social conflict, so to speak, by treating that as fact which is not fact, namely, the purposes which are struggling to be fact.

In this respect, its object might be stated in Kant's language. "So act," runs another of his formulations of the categorical imperative, "as to treat humanity, whether in thine own person or in that of any other, in every case as an end withal, never as means only."[4] Wherever we find purposes, we ought to treat them as ends; that is, make them part of our own ends.

Perhaps this is what is meant when it is said that we must found our moral and political theory on respect for the dignity of the individual. We must not treat the individual as mere fact, but must take his purposes seriously. That is, we may not treat the individual as a purely existential being, but must respect that about him which transcends his immediate existence and which makes him a rational and a social animal.

Even in the more civilized societies, instances of perfect reconciliation are rare. Yet in the events of ordinary family and business life, as well as in the larger problems of society, we can find approximations.[5] The need for reconciliation in social conflicts and the ways in which it can be fostered have been emphasized in the writings of one of the keenest of modern students of politics, E. P. Herring. For example, in his *Presidential Leadership*, he points out how useful the administrative branch of government can be in reconciling social and economic differences before these differences reach the legislative assembly where factors of prestige, politics, and limited time and information may hinder an integration of opposing points of view. He notes the familiar fact that the pressure of interested groups often disrupts the formation of a truly national policy, but he doubts that a reform of the mechanics of government, such as strengthening the executive, will solve the problem. He observes that it is no solution to frustrate certain groups merely in order to make lawmaking move more smoothly. For the only real solution is to examine carefully the interests of the conflicting groups and to find a policy which, so far as possible, reconciles these interests. Here the administrative branch working through committees representing government, experts, and interested groups can make a great contribution.

He writes: "Giving the president formal powers for overruling Congress offers no solution any more than would procedural dodges for increasing Congressional authority. Appealing to the general electorate to decide between the two fails to meet the real question. The crux of the matter is adjustment. This calls for *expertise* exercised with patience and subtlety; it calls for the highest intelligence in the discovery of new ways and means. You cannot settle a technical question of engineering by a show of hands; questions of human engineering are no less intricate."[6]

The business of solving such problems is one which must be shared in some measure by those who are involved in the difficulties and who must carry out the terms of the agreement. They are the ones who know the important facts, that is, the "internal" facts about the purposes to be reconciled. Any one of them may seize upon that creative hypothesis, or make a suggestion which will contribute to the formulation of that hypothesis, which solves the problem. In this kind of problem-solving, the stage of reflection is a stage of discussion. It is the reflection of men together about their common problems. At this point, the ethics of civilization involves the principle of democracy.

A. D. Lindsay has described this kind of thinking, which is both collective and creative, in a striking passage in his *Essentials of Democracy*. "When men who are serving a common purpose," he writes, "meet to pool their experience, to air their difficulties and even their discontents, there comes about a real process of collective thinking. The narrowness and one-sidedness of each person's point of view are corrected, and something emerges which each can recognize as embodying the truth of what he stood for, and yet (or rather therefore) is seen to serve the purpose of the society better than what any one conceived for himself. That is of course an ideal. Such perfect agreement is not often reached. But it is an ideal which is always to some extent realized when there is open and frank discussion . . .

"Observe further that the moment we take discussions seriously, we are committed to the view that we are concerned not primarily to obtain or register consent, but to find something out . . . The root of the matter is that if the discussion is at all successful, we discover something from it which could have been discovered in no other way."[7]

In the process of reconciliation, a group discovers its common purpose. It may already be united in some bonds of community. Reconciliation, by obliging it to adjust and add to its purposes, enlarges and strengthens these bonds. In short, a group finds its common purpose, not by speculating on the moral code it ought to follow, nor by a search for a pre-existing set of natural laws. Rather it finds that purpose by solving the problems which the conflicts of man and nature, and man and man, set before it. In this process the common purpose and moral code of the group is created and developed. Tension between man and man, like tension between man and nature, is a source of growth. Our ideal is to eliminate both kinds of tension. Yet if, *per impossibile*, we were to succeed, the sources of creative advance would be stopped up.

The ethics of civilization, as sketched here, it seems to me, makes some progress toward bringing to light the larger notions which lie behind our moral feelings. It is a duty of the individual to develop his own skills and powers. It is also his duty to seek constantly to bring these gifts to the service of a common purpose. The ideal is a community in which the happiness of each integrally involves the happiness of all. The principles of the intelligent inquiry are principles of reason. So also are the principles of community and reconciliation. In this sense, the larger notion underlying the ethics of civilization may be said to be the idea of reason.

*The Good Will and the Beautiful Soul*   There are many difficulties which come to mind when one tries to state this theory of ethics more precisely and to picture how it might be put into practice. However, it does plausibly meet the objection which was raised at the start of this discussion of ethics: it is not too concrete. It does not set up one type of economy—a subsistence or a profit-making or a socialist economy—as the one model to which all societies, regardless of time or place, must try to conform. It does not put the stamp of approval on a particular pattern of sexual relations between men and women as the only permissible one and condemn all others, regardless of circumstance. It accords very well with this theory that particular moral codes should be relative to time and place and that they should change in the course of history.

From the general ideal of this ethics by itself, no conclusions follow which direct what a man or a society ought to do. There must, so to speak, be a minor premise stating the facts in the widest sense about that man or that society. Given these, the ideal of this ethics provides rules of procedure which can lead to concrete decisions. It is formal, yet not as formal as the pure community theory which could permit decisions which run counter to some of our deeper moral feelings.

Let us examine the bearing of this ethics on the problem of purpose. As we noted before, there is in our common feelings about morality an intimation of an answer to our question. It is that men ought to conform their purposes to the moral law, regardless of consequences; that somehow the weighing of consequences is not to affect us in doing our duty. Such an intimation is hardly clear. If we take it to mean that a man can decide what he ought to do without giving thought to the probable consequences of his act, surely the notion is impractical. In outlining the ethics of civilization we have been stating in general terms what a man should try to accomplish in the world, that is, through the consequences of his acts. For instance, in trying to reconcile the parties to some social conflict, he must rely on experience to suggest to him the particular operations and means which are likely to work in this kind of situation. The ethical ideal cannot itself suggest such means; yet without them he cannot act in any determinate way. They must be derived from experience and can only be a knowledge of probabilities.

Knowledge of probable consequences will inevitably enter into purpose. Yet we can still accept the intimation of our moral feelings that consequences are not what count. The idea is something like this: The "good will," the purpose, aiming at what appear to be probably the best consequences under the circumstances, is somehow justified in itself, even though the intended consequences do not actually follow. That is, men ought to attempt what experience suggests is the best way of promoting civilization, although they can have no certainty of what their attempt will lead to. In fact, our efforts may have some strange and even horrifying results. Our great labors may bring forth mice; many of us may die in vain. Yet comic or tragic as the results may be, morality affirms our justification. What counts is not the consequence, but the state of the soul. "Nothing," wrote Kant, "can possibly be conceived in the world, or even out of it, which can be called good without qualification, except a Good Will."[8]

Here is a possible solution to the problem of purpose. It is different from the answer of the instrumentalist. His answer was to take purpose at its face value and to claim that with "enough" knowledge, man could control the world and make his history. The problem of purpose arose when we tried to accept this answer. Here in our discussion of ethical theory we have come upon a different approach. Following this approach, we do not rest our defense of purpose on the vain hope that it can certainly attain what it proposes. We allow for the fundamental pluralism and unexpected discontinuities of the world. We hold that there is a justification for purpose beyond the actual consequences.

Dewey's final view sometimes seems to be remarkably similar. As we have seen, no one is more acutely aware than he of the unpredictable flux of things. It is not strange, therefore, if his ultimate justification of intelligent purpose is far from a crude instrumentalism. "And upon the very most hopeful outlook," he writes, "study and planning are more important in the meaning, the enrichment of content, which they add to present activity, than is the increase of control they effect . . . The good, satisfaction, 'end,' of growth of present action in shades and scope of meaning is the only good within our control, and the only one, accordingly, for which responsibility exists. The rest is luck, fortune."[9]

This is not instrumentalism, but what might be called aesthetic humanism. When knowledge grows, it is to be valued, not essentially as an instrument of control, but as an immediate joy. And surely we cannot entirely reject this theory of the "beautiful soul." To found your plans upon a wide examination of the facts; to integrate into purpose your understanding of the purposes of others; to find the unity of mind in judgment springing from a great complexity in deliberation, is to take an immediate pleasure in the beauties of civilized intelligence.

The civilized soul is a value in itself. It is an aesthetic value and we ought to try to be civilized because that is aesthetically the pleasantest way to live. It is a moral value and we ought to try to be civilized—simply because we ought. With these conclusions we must feel a warm sympathy. But will the mind for long be content with them? Can you seriously grant the hypothesis of pluralism and, as an aesthetic or moral humanist, still take purpose seriously? For does not pluralism destroy the distinction between one purpose and another? If pluralism is the final word on the nature of fact, then "anything is possible, even the most impossible and most senseless." And if anything is possible; if any strange and unexpected result may follow from any purpose, then there is no real difference between one purpose and another.

Purposes purport to perform a function in experience. If you cut them off from the future, destroy their functional character, reduce them to mere contents, then you have eliminated what makes one purpose different from another. And if there is no serious distinction between one purpose and another how can the mind decide that one purpose is more civilized than another?

Meanings which may or may not lead to certain future facts are mere fancies. They are what the skeptics and materialists have always said they were, mere *voces*, affections of the present moment whose reference to the future is an illusion produced on men by chance. The humanist or moralist who will occupy himself with trying to collect such sterile tokens of human credulity must himself be a little blind. Aesthetic pleasure or moral compulsion cannot stand against the pluralism of the world. The world's chaos invades our inner thoughts about the world and destroys order and distinction there in accord with their destruction in the external world. Purpose will lack a defense until we find some reason to believe that it really bears fruit and that the blind forces do not rule.

Ethical theory makes a promising suggestion when it says that in a sense we must overlook the pluralism of the world. It makes a promising suggestion when it says that what counts is not success, but the state of the soul. It makes a promising suggestion, *if* it says that the civilized, sympathetic soul does somehow bear fruit. But how and where does it bear fruit? Can we believe that the discords and failures which we meet with are apparent, not real, and that these apparent evils are superseded in some vaster continuum? Could this vaster continuum be the stream of history? In the next chapter, we shall examine this suggestion.

## CHAPTER SEVEN

# PHILOSOPHY OF HISTORY
# AGAINST ITSELF

THERE IS A TENDENCY FOR HUMAN PURPOSE TO PROSPER AND DE-
velop. It is only a tendency and the facts have prevented us
from calling it a law. But not many years ago, as people understood the facts, they found it logical to believe that history was
governed by a law of growth and accumulation. Many believed in the inevitability of progress.

This belief saved them from the problem of discontinuity.
A belief in progress obliged them to admit the relativity of
truth, but at the same time it cured the principal difficulty
issuing from this doctrine. For, according to the theory of
progress, the unbroken growth of the world is paralleled by
an unbroken growth of our knowledge of the world. Hence,
while the knowledge of one period will be altered by being
augmented, it will never be diminished. What is true in one
period remains true thereafter, although subject to reinterpretation. Today, however, we find untenable the premise
on which this happy conclusion is founded and so the relativity
of truth means for us that sooned or later our present knowledge will unexpectedly lead to frustration or disaster.

We might speak of this effect of the passing of the belief
in progress as a breakdown of "philosophy of history." The
fathers of philosophy of history, Kant, Hegel, and Marx, believed in progress. Modern philosophers of history do not, and
thereby open their theories to a crushing objection.

For the doctrine of the relativity of truth, which philosophy
of history so convincingly documents, now turns upon philosophy of history itself. If any body of truth is relative to a
certain kind of society and a certain period of history, what

shall we say of the truths which constitute our philosophy of history?[1] If, like other truths, they are relative, then they will describe the movement of society only during a certain period of history. When that period comes to an end, the truths of this philosophy of history will cease to work. They will become as out-of-date as mercantilism or laisser-faire economics, and the consequences which will flow from trying to apply them will be as unplanned and possibly unpleasant as the French Revolution or the Great Depression.

In short, any philosophy of history is a piece of knowledge. If the fundamental pluralism and discontinuity of the world make any knowledge an unreliable instrument, then they also make any philosophy of history unreliable as a means of prediction or planning. This is merely an application of the general conclusion of irrationalism.

These remarks anticipate the conclusions of this chapter. We shall proceed toward those conclusions *via* an examination of the Marxist variety of philosophy of history. We shall first consider a conception of the central theme of history which Marxism shares with a large class of philosophies of history. This is the conception that history is the story of man's struggle with nature, a struggle in which at once he wins concrete freedom and a civilized character. Then we shall go on to examine the peculiarly Marxist view of how political policies are governed by social interests, contrasting that with a democratic view founded upon the theory of creative intelligence. Finally, we shall consider more particularly the belief in progress which is at the heart of Marxist teleology.

*The Struggle for Concrete Freedom*   In a familiar passage in the *Anti-Dühring*, Engels has described that great theme of history as the struggle for concrete freedom. "Hegel," he writes, "was the first to state correctly the relation between freedom and necessity. To him, freedom is the appreciation of necessity. 'Necessity is *blind* only *in so far as it is not under-*

*stood.*' Freedom does not consist in the dream of independence of natural laws, but in the knowledge of these laws, and in the possibility this gives of systematically making them work towards definite ends. This holds good in relation to the laws of external nature and to those which govern the bodily and mental life of men themselves—two classes of laws which we can separate from each other at most only in thought but not in reality . . .

"Freedom therefore consists in the control over ourselves and over external nature which is founded on knowledge of natural necessity; it is therefore necessarily a product of historical development. The first men who separated themselves from the animal kingdom were in all essentials as unfree as the animals themselves, but each step forward in civilization was a step toward freedom. On the threshold of human history stands the discovery that mechanical motion can be transformed into heat, the production of fire by friction; at the close of the development so far gone through stands the discovery that heat can be transformed into mechanical motion: the steam engine."[2]

Men struggle to conquer nature and in so doing they acquire a knowledge of the blind forces of nature which renders these forces no longer blind. So far as we plan and make our history we are concretely free. Hence, the underlying theme of the growth of civilization is the struggle for power, knowledge, freedom—"the endless progressive evolution of humanity" which flows from our pursuit of "an exhaustive knowledge of the world system in all its interrelations."[3]

The notion that this struggle for concrete freedom is the central theme of history was common in the nineteenth century. For example, in a penetrating essay, *Fate*, Emerson considers it as part of the "ascending effort" of the Universe. He recites the limitation which circumstance and "law" put upon us, calling this limitation "Fate." Then he continues:

"We can afford to allow the limitation, if we know it is the meter of the growing man.. We stand against Fate as children stand up against the wall in their father's house, and notch their height from year to year. But when the boy grows to man, and is master of the house, he pulls down that wall, and builds a new and bigger. 'Tis only a question of time. Every brave youth is in training to ride and rule this dragon. His science is to make weapons and wings of these passions and retarding forces . . .

"Fate, then, is a name for facts not yet passed under the fire of thought;—for causes which are unpenetrated . . . The water drowns ship and sailor, like a grain of dust. But learn to swim, trim your bark, and the wave which drowned it, will be cloven by it, and carry it, like its own foam, a plume and a power . . ."[4]

*Marxist Determinism*   The central theme of history according to Marxist doctrine is the growth of concrete freedom. But how does this growth come about? Can men sometimes think up solutions to their problems, lighting on hypotheses which enable them to subdue nature by obeying her, working out schemes of coöperation which reconcile conflicts of purpose? Or can they only register in their plans and purposes those new facts of nature and those new forms of social organization which the blind forces of history present to them? It is not easy to get general agreement on "what Marx really meant." Yet it seems to be that it is of the essence of the Marxist theory of determinism that it chooses the second of these alternatives.

A well-known passage in *The German Ideology* by Marx and Engels runs as follows: "We set out from real, active men, and on the basis of their real life-process we demonstrate the development of the ideological reflexes and echoes of this life-process. The phantoms formed in the human brain are also, necessarily, sublimates of their material life-process, which is empirically verifiable and bound to material premises. Morality, religion, metaphysics, all the rest of ideology and their corresponding forms of consciousness, thus no longer retain the semblance of independence. They have no history, no development; but men, developing their material production and their material intercourse, alter along with this their real existence, their thinking and the product of their thinking. Life is not determined by consciousness, but consciousness by life."[5]

This is a rather general statement. But it is clear that when it comes to social problems and conflicts, human intelligence, according to Marxist doctrine, is wholly uncreative. In the *Anti-Dühring* Engels writes that "the means through which the abuses [of capitalism] that have been revealed can be got rid of must . . . be present, in more or less developed form, in the altered conditions of production. These means are not to be *invented* by the mind, but *discovered* by means of the mind in the existing material facts of production."[6] "When people speak of ideas that revolutionize society," wrote Marx in the *Communist Manifesto*, "they do but express the fact, that within the old society the elements of a new one have been created, and that the dissolution of the old ideas keeps even pace with the dissolution of the old conditions of existence."[7]

For instance, the bourgeoisie rose out of the medieval trading class without anyone planning it that way. The blind consequences of many people's acts created that mode of production and exchange which is called bourgeois and which is marked especially by the exchange of goods for profit, as described by Marx in *Capital*. The people who conducted this mode of production realized what they were doing only after their mode of production had come into existence. Then and only then did they understand what they were doing and consciously try to promote their interest. Again, the modern proletariat came into existence quite unintentionally with the growth of large cities and factory production. Thereafter, they perceived their condition and their interest, and became class-conscious.

It is enormously important how we answer this question whether thought is creative. For one thing, it is only if we assume that it is creative, that democracy makes sense. Democracy, the attempt to settle conflicts by discussion, makes sense only if we assume that reflection in individual minds and the group reflection which takes place in discussion, can hit on creative hypotheses. If discussion in parliamentary assemblies, if public debate and private reflection can do no more than register conformally an already existing interest or conflict of interests, then there is no sense whatever in such practices —except as propaganda.

The Marxist theory does not hold that men are governed by certain fixed and inflexible drives or instincts. On the contrary, it insists that the given elements of human nature can be and have been manifested in many different ways and that as human knowledge and power grow there is enrichment and growth of human nature, "the endless progressive evolution of humanity." "By . . . acting on the external world and changing it," writes Marx, man "at the same time changes his own nature. He develops the potentialities that slumber within him, and subjects these inner forces to his own control." [8]

Neither does the theory expound a brand of social mechanism. The mark of a mechanistic theory of society is that it holds that history is uncreative, being governed by a finite set of laws and manifesting a finite set of predicates; that history continually repeats itself like the movement of heavenly bodies in the Newtonian universe. But the Marxist "laws" are laws of endless creation.

On those points the Marxist theory is in harmony with the rationalist views presented in this essay. The divergence comes when the Marxist theory denies a share in this power of creativity to human reflection and consequently to social discussion. It follows from this denial that, when a conflict of purposes arises, there is no hope of settling it by discussion or taking thought, individually or collectively. Chance, of course, may settle it without open conflict, as chance in observations may reveal to a scientific investigator an important discovery. Otherwise the conflict will break into the open, each party treating the other not as purpose, but as mere fact, until conquest by one or the other restores equilibrium.

*The Dialectical Process*    However, according to Marxist theory this conflict is not fundamentally destructive. The only things destroyed are certain institutions of repression. The technics, in the broadest sense, of the old society continue on in the new. For instance, the great corporate monopolies of late capitalism will not be destroyed by the workers, but will merely be taken over by them and managed, not according to the self-contradictory system of production for profit, but according to the new system of production for use which the trade unions already have brought into existence in embryo.

This accumulation of social technics from stage to stage without essential loss is the dialectical process. In this process the conflict between the old society and the revolutionary class—between "thesis" and "antithesis"—does not end in the destruction of one or the other, but in a new society which embraces the characteristics of both elements—the "synthesis." The thesis and antithesis are neither contraries nor contradictories in the sense in which these terms are used in Aristotelian logic. For in that case they would be mutually exclusive. They are rather "opposites" in the Hegelian sense; that is, diverse factors which yet combine in a real unity.

That diverse elements often do join together to make a new unity is a notion which, as we have seen, considerable evidence supports. Dewey's means-consequence relation embodies this principle and when in the next Part we examine Whitehead's theory of nature we shall find that this principle is fundamental to his doctrine of creative advance.

What is being pointed out here is the peculiar use which Marxist theory makes of the dialectical principle. This theory holds that history is divided into stages in which one form of society succeeds another dialectically. That succession, in other words, is not the succession of a series of different and mutually exclusive elements. Like the means-consequence relation, it is a creative and cumulative process in which each new stage includes and goes beyond the previous one.

Here is the heart of the Marxist faith in progress. Here also is the doctrine which saves the Marxist denial of creativity to human thought from leading to pessimism. Marxism holds that mind can only register conformally what fact presents to it. Mind cannot invent, but only discover, new social patterns and practices. If there is change in history, that is not because a mind or a parliamentary assembly planned it that way. All that such agencies can do is enable men to repeat what they already are doing. Where change occurs it is because of the unplanned, blind consequences of their acts, for example, the creation of the great city, the rise of the modern proletariat, the recurrence of depressions during late capitalism. But thanks to the dialectical process these blind consequences invariably lead not to destruction and loss, but to social growth. The revolutions which mark the passage from one stage to another are not fundamentally destructive. They alter and finally eliminate certain organs of repression which the Marxists call the "state," but the essential knowledge and social technics of the old order continue on in the new.

*Politics and Social Interests*  Marxist theory holds, first, that conflicts of social interests can be settled, not by reflection and discussion, but only by violence; and secondly, that the violence of such conflicts is not fundamentally destructive, but progressive. Given these two assumptions, it is not hard to see why Marxist theorists should sing the praises of violence, of "the iron broom of history." We shall better understand the Marxist theory if we contrast it briefly with one view of the liberal-democratic tradition.

In social conflicts the contending parties may simply persist in their old habits and refuse to take thought together. When a parliamentary assembly, for instance, becomes the battle ground for interests which are inflexible in their demands, then the hope of a creative solution vanishes. In such a case, politics merely registers the conflicts of interests in society, but does nothing to solve them, except as the conquest of one over the other may be regarded as a solution.

However, this is not by any means always the case in political controversy. Suppose we grant that representatives in parliamentary bodies usually represent a certain interest or set of interests. We must still admit that discussion around and in parliamentary bodies often enables these representatives to get a more enlightened view of what their particular interests require in the way of government policy. It may enable them to see a common interest which they have with other interests, but which they had not seen before; it may enable them to work out new arrangements constituting a new common interest. In both ways representatives and factions, which at the outset of discussion were in conflict, may come to agreement.

This outline of a defense of democratic methods does not rest on a belief that people will, or should, act against their own self-interest. It does not say that democracy works only when groups surrender their self-interest to the general good. It holds merely that discussion may enable conflicting groups to come to agreement by giving them a more enlightened view of the means to their ends. Indeed, it would hold that a general good which did not include the self-interests of its parts was a fraud.

People sometimes say with a sneer or a sigh that political policies "reflect" social interests and that parliamentary bodies are the battle ground where contending interests pursue their objects. We can admit this and still be far from giving up democracy and falling into the arms of the Marxist. A democrat may admit this, or indeed insist on it. But he also insists that the representative process can be creative, that the struggle of interests when taken from the market place to the talking shop fairly often gives rise to a policy which embodies the demands of the interests and yet goes beyond them to state a public interest. What he denies is the Marxist view that these policies merely conform to the interests behind them and that the struggle of interests in democratic discussions can be no more than a disguised form of civil war.

If the view sketched here is a fair version, so far as it goes, of the liberal-democratic tradition then its points of agreement and disagreement with Marxism are clear. With Marxist theory this present version of liberalism would agree that the great theme of history is the struggle for concrete freedom. In this respect it would find more affinity with Marxism than with some other versions of liberalism. It would hold, for instance, that the Marxist conception of the infinite progress of human knowledge is far more satisfying than the program of the champions of the Consumptive State whose utmost dream of the destiny of man goes not one jot beyond Mr. Hoover's "two cars in every garage."

The divergence of the present version of liberalism from Marxist theory is emphatic. It springs from the Marxist insistence on the futility of discussion and the need and inevitability of violence. This is the point where the liberal, old or new, must refuse to go along with the Marxist. It is the point where the theory of democracy diverges from the doctrine of class struggle and violent revolution. This divergence follows from the fact that one doctrine accepts, the other rejects, a belief in the creativity of human intelligence.

*Determinism, Economic and Dialectical*  We reject the Marxist doctrine that political policies will conform identically with social interests already in existence. We deny that political policies cannot alter creatively the institutions through which the struggle with nature is carried on. We assert that political planning can do more than slavishly try to preserve the status quo.

The doctrine which we reject, it seems to me, is the heart of the Marxist variety of "economic" determinism. However, we must distinguish this doctrine from another branch of Marxist theory which is often spoken of as part of Marxist determinism. This is the theory of the dialectical process, that is, the cumulative succession of freer, more civilized, more productive societies.

In what sense can you call a theory deterministic which holds, as Marxism does, that the processes of history are truly creative? One clear sense of the word determinism we have already discussed. It is determinism in the sense of causal conformation, to use a phrase of Whitehead's. Now in the dialectical process there is a measure of such determinism, since the later stages of history include the characteristics of the earlier stages. However, each succeeding stage, each new society, also goes beyond the previous ones, and constitutes a genuine historical creation.

Since this new society never existed before in history, there remains only one sense in which it could have been determined. It may have have been determined in that it came from "outside history"; that is, in the sense that it was the actualization of an idea or purpose. If the processes of history are not deterministic in the conformal sense, then they may yet be deterministic in the teleological sense.

According to such a view, the new entities in history follow from the real possibilities of the elements which came together to make them. Some of these possibilities may have been actualized before in the world. But the unique character of an entity proceeds from the real potentiality of its antecedents to come together as this entity.

These are notions which we shall examine in the next Part. Here it can at least be emphasized that determinism of the teleological variety is something very different from that of the conformal variety. It should hardly be called determinism, for it is consistent with freedom, in the sense of creativity. The new entities which occur in such a process have not occurred before. Their coming into existence really accomplishes something and adds something—which had to be added.

*Marxist transcendentalism*    This kind of determinism has a transcendentalist sound. But is it so far from Marxism? How, for instance, can a Marxist talk about the future (as he continually does) unless he believes in something transcendental? Here before him are the "given" facts of the present world. He will not find the future among them. Then what is he talking about when he speaks of the future? What do his words "refer" to? Surely not to anything he can clearly perceive. But the Marxist future is not just a mere tomorrow. It is an inevitably progressive future. The dialectical process is not just a tendency of history; it is the *law* of history. What can this mean except what transcendental optimists have always meant, namely, that an Infinite Purpose surely manifests itself in the affairs of men? At the heart of the dialectical process, we find that Absolute Idea or Purpose which Hegel said was unfolding in the world, but which the founders of Marxism contemptuously professed to have got rid of.

Of course, Marxists have always insisted that they were "materialists," that the "ultimate reality" of the objective world is "matter." But these are words. What kind of "matter" can they be said to believe in when their theory goes on to endow it with the properties of "mind"? Materialism, as a theory of nature, has commonly been taken to mean that the fundamental entities of the world are separate, impenetrable, and wholly without internal relations. Above all, it means that the world excludes purpose or design; what happens, happens, but you cannot account for it on the ground of a preëxisting plan. The Marxist rejects this brand of materialism as nondialectical.[9] The properties which he finds in the world include cumulation, creativity, and purpose. A world so characterized is hardly a materialistic world.

The underlying faith in a Purpose which guarantees sheer progress in the affairs of men is of the essence of Marxism. It is one element in the intense contrast which this theory makes between the impotence of man and the grandeur of his destiny. There are many theories which promise man a heavenly consummation, but usually they also insist that his own efforts and decisions have a small, but integral, part in bringing about that end.

In Marxist theory one of these elements is exaggerated, the other depreciated. The Heaven which is promised mankind is not mysterious and hidden, but is, and will be, infinitely unfolded before our eyes. There is a single continuum of human history within which the infinite and unbroken progress of the race takes place. At the same time, this progress is wholly the work of the blind forces. Human thought is not in the slightest creative, but merely registers the growing advance of knowledge, power, and freedom.

*Problem of relativity and postulate of Progress*  This faith in progress is also that element in the theory which at once raises the problem of the relativity of truth and opens a way by which Marxism may save itself from self-destruction at the hands of this doctrine. It creates that problem because, from a belief in the infinite progress of human knowledge, it follows that what we know at any particular time is small and inadequate when compared with all that is to be known. Obviously, if you are going to hold out to man a great future for investigating society and nature, you are obliged implicitly to disparage his present state of enlightenment.

Science, writes Engels in the *Anti-Dühring*, seeks "the formulation in thought of an exact picture of the world system in which we live." But it is impossible that we should ever get such a formulation. For, he continues, "if at any time in the evolution of mankind such a final, conclusive system of the interconnections within the world—physical as well as mental and historical—were brought to completion, this would mean that human knowledge had reached its limit, and, from the moment when society had been brought into accord with that system, further historical evolution would be cut short—which would be an absurd idea, pure nonsense. Mankind therefore finds itself faced with a contradiction: on the one hand, it has to gain an exhaustive knowledge of the world system in all its interrelations; and on the other hand, because of the nature both of man and of the world system, this task can never be completely fulfilled."[10] Which contradiction, he goes on to say, is "the main lever of all intellectual advance."

Again, he writes farther along in the *Anti-Dühring*, while discussing the growth of concrete freedom: "But how young the whole of human history still is, and how ridiculous it would be to attempt to ascribe any absolute validity to our present views, is evident from the simple fact that all past history can be characterised as the history of the epoch from the practical discovery of the transformation of mechanical motion into heat up to that of the transformation of heat into mechanical motion."[11]

The problem is this: If all knowledge is relative to a certain society or class, then what of Marxism? Shall we ascribe "absolute validity" to its theory of the past, present, and future? Its predictions like all predictions are founded upon partial knowledge and hence may or may not come true. Here the Marxist practice of "psychologizing" its opponents has been turned on Marxism. The outcome is a doubt of all knowledge and prediction, the Marxist variety included.

In this way the notion that history is progressive raises the problem of the relativity of truth. However, as that notion is stated in the Marxist theory, it opens a possible way of solving the problem, although at the cost of grossly violating the facts.

According to Marxist theory there is sheer progress and accumulation as each new social synthesis includes and goes beyond the preceding society. If you hold that history, as fact, is wholly progressive, you may also argue that the truth which is founded upon the facts of one period will also hold good in a later period, although in an unpredictable context. Your predictions will not describe the whole of the future, but neither will they describe anything which is excluded from that future. They will be incomplete, but not incompatible with the facts.

Consequently, you might maintain that while Marxism as a body of truth will continually be transformed as history accumulates, no part of it will fail to hold good, although the whole will be continually added to and reinterpreted. In this way, for instance, you might say the original doctrine of Marx has been reinterpreted, but not contradicted, by Lenin's theory of imperialism and Palme Dutt's theory of fascism.

The idea can be applied to the question with which the previous chapter ended. The life-course of an individual, of a nation, of a whole social system may seem senseless because of the discontinuities of history and nature. The truth held by a man or group or age sometimes works, and sometimes does not. Therefore, it appears, as the skeptic suggests, that truth never really does the work; that purpose is radically cut off from consequence. But all this is only appearance, according to the postuate of progress accepted by Marxism. Particular truths in history, and the men and institutions they inform, seem to fail, but in reality they do not. Nothing important is really lost. The relative truths of individuals and societies live on in ever wider syntheses and are fulfilled in the vaster continuum of advancing civilization.

*History a problem, not a solution* The postulate of progress may make Marxism internally consistent in regard to this problem. But it also makes that theory, and any other philosophy of history which accepts it, a travesty of the facts. Let us waive the sophisticated objection that even if all past history had been pure progress, there would still be lacking grounds for predicting what the future would be. For the simple fact is that past history has not been pure progress and accumulation from synthesis to wider synthesis. Great civilizations have come into existence, flourished mightily, and then suffered decadence and destruction, passing on to later ages only fragments of their culture.

Sometimes we can explain apparent destruction by showing how there has been growth and the formation of a new synthesis. But sometimes we cannot explain destruction away. In the history of the race as in personal experience, there are terrible incompatibilities which are followed not by creation but by destruction. "History," as Reinhold Niebuhr once said in a sermon, "does not solve problems; history is a problem."

History is our problem. Or perhaps it is better to use a broader term and say that experience is our problem. The problem of experience is that it is discontinuous. Within it, as within the history of cultures, there are periods of growth. Then there is decay or sudden extinction. What follows bears only traces, few or many, or perhaps even none, of what went before. There is not just one single continuum of ever-increasing progress and growth. There are many continua; a multi-verse, not a universe. That at any rate is the common sense of it: everything is infected with mortality. So far as experience or history can tell us, pluralism is the last word. That is, death is the last word.

In our more naïve states of mind, we may be unaware of this. Children sometimes act as if nothing could harm them; as if they were immortal. Whole societies sometimes get in the simple-minded condition of thinking that nothing can ever bring to an end their prosperity and those peculiar methods by which they pursue it.

The philosopher of history may construct some majestic scheme of progress, purporting to show how there has been a steady growth in the power and knowledge of Western man. But it is impossible to overlook the hideous waste. Cultures, arts, ideas, have come into existence and been trampled out leaving only faint traces on succeeding generations. Our historical reconstructions give us hints of what those lost ages were like. But even the best history is a kind of taxidermy.

With these few bones and old feathers we make an image, but it will never fly.

Can we expect any more of the future than we know of the past? We must hold that the truths possessed by these dead peoples and cultures were only contingent, only possible. That is, they could, and did, hold of fact; but they were not certainties; they held only for "a time." Are we then to say that our truths, for the first time in history, are certainties? That they cannot prove false? That our society cannot perish?

Experience affords us little ground for answering "yes." But if you grant that your truths, your best truths, are contingent, how can you take them seriously? How, when you are faced with alternative ways of acting or predicting, can you decide between them? For they are all simply possibilities and the fact that your experience leads to one as the "most probable" is close to insignificant.

What we must have is a defense of our best knowledge. We must have some reason for acting on the "most probable" knowledge of consequences; for banishing the suggestion that in the end it is all a matter of luck, chance, accident. That is the problem of irrationalism: the lack of a reason to trust our own best knowledge and science.

In a sense, what we need is a defense of experience against itself. There is such a defense. But, as we shall see, it also springs from experience. What we need is a deeper empiricism, a deeper pragmatism than has yet appeared.

### PART THREE

# THEODICY

## CHAPTER EIGHT

# ONE POWER OR MANY?

THE PROBLEM IS: WHAT WILL THE FUTURE DO TO OUR PLANS
and the things which we have already created through them?
This is not just a problem which touches the planner or the
student of history. It is one of the commonest feelings of men:
Where am I going? What is the meaning of my present job,
of my life, of the society and nation of which I am a member?
When we look back we are balked on all sides by limits to
our knowledge of origins and of the causes and roots of present events; our knowledge of history and nature is never exhaustive. Beyond these limits lies a mere It, a Something
whence we sprang. When we look forward, we find another
such limit immediately before us. Our fate even in the next
moment is uncertain. What happens to us depends, not only
upon our intentions, but also upon the blind forces of history
and nature, upon the It or Something which is the world we
never made. These tender hopes and plans of youth, what
will the objective world do to them? This confident round
of habits and institutions on which our society sets its bless-
ing, can it survive the blows of reality? These creations of
our civilization, what place will history have for them?
    What is this source from which things appear and into
which they disappear? Is it chaos: the senseless clash of many
isolated and incompatible centers of being? Or is it an order:
a something which in part preserves and corresponds to the
lesser, transient orders of my existence and my society? In all
ages and in various moods, practical and poetic, emotional and
dryly intellectualist, men have asked this question. In it lies
that wonder which Plato held to be the beginning of philosophy. From it also issues that not ignoble fear, which some
have regarded as the beginning of wisdom.

A nameless thegn of Edwin, king of Northumbria in the seventh century, stated this question in an unforgettable image. Bede records his words spoken at a witan of 627 A.D. at which the king was converted to Christianity.

"The present life of man, O king," he said, "seems to me, in comparison of that time which is unknown to us, like to the swift flight of a sparrow through the room wherein you sit at supper in winter with your commanders and ministers, and a good fire in the midst, whilst the storms of rain and snow prevail abroad; the sparrow, I say, flying in at one door and immediately out at another, whilst he is within, is safe from the wintry storm; but after a short space of fair weather, he immediately vanishes out of your sight, into the dark winter from which he had emerged. So this life of man appears for a short space, but of what went before or of what is to follow, we are utterly ignorant. If, therefore, this new doctrine contains something more certain, it seems justly to deserve to be followed."[1]

Here is the primordial experience and problem of philosophy. To be conscious is to have plans and purposes to which we struggle to make the unknown future conform. To be conscious that this is what we are doing, that is, to be self-conscious; to ask the question, "What is the status of our knowledge and purposes over against this Other?" is to ask the first question of philosophy. No matter how narrowly we may state the problem of purpose, on thought it will soon reveal the outlines of this larger question.

Men ask this question because it is forced on them by experience. Yet it must be admitted that it is not inevitable that a man should ask this question or feel the wonder and fear which it may inspire. A child does not, and that is part of its charm. For a child, the simple set of means and consequences which it understands seems to exhaust the possibilities of the universe. In its naïveté there is something of omniscience.

One might erect naïveté into a first principle. One might say that in experience he finds only the "given"—certain plain, unadulterated facts. To talk about something beyond these facts which somehow is, and which is yet unknown, is to talk nonsense. Why conjure up a noumenon behind this phenomenon? If you have perceived something, then by that token you know what it is. If you have not perceived it, then you know nothing about it and so cannot say that it is.

This view may sound nonsensical, yet there is a tendency for thinkers to try to find a resting place in it, safe from the tortured controversies of reflective thought. The skeptic, for instance, sometimes adopts this position. He may deny that we perceive that there is a source from which our perceptions originate and to which they refer and which is yet different from them. It follows that to speak of that which lies beyond what you have clearly perceived is to talk nonsense.

The positivist habit of mind also inclines to fall into this brand of naïveté. The positivist records what he has clearly seen and will say nothing more about the matter. Indeed, he is so concerned with the clear parts of experience that he gets to the point of denying there are any vague parts. He would like to solve our problem by denying that it exists.

This is undoubtedly an ingenious suggestion. If only we could get people to accept it, it would banish an enormous sum of worry and troubled thought from the world. Whatever happened to us as practical men or scientific investigators; whatever we perceived clearly, we should accept as fact. So far as we concerned ourselves about the future, we should do so only on the expectation that it would be like the clearly perceived past.

Such a mood would put an end to that amount of scientific inquiry which starts from the belief that one can know that there is something unknown and that, therefore, inquiry may be worth while. It would no doubt also make our statesmen and men of practical affairs either unduly complacent, if the past as they saw it had been full of good fortune; or else quite desperate, if they viewed the past as unhappy. Still who can deny that in a sense such ignorance would be bliss?

There is no single way of stating the problem of purpose. Practical men, poets, historians, philosophers, all have their peculiar way of stating and, if possible, solving it. Within the intricately wrought debates of philosophy itself the question takes many forms. For the person interested in planning, the most striking form is the problem of prediction or induction: "the divination of some characteristics of a particular future from the known characteristics of a particular past."[2] Our discussion should have enabled us to see why, in Whitehead's words, "the theory of Induction is the despair of philosophy."[3]

The problem can also be stated as a problem of epistemology: What is the relation of subject and object, of knower and known? Or, in various forms, as a problem of ethics: Can men in any sense be held responsible for their acts, or are they at the mercy of blind forces? Can men achieve any concrete freedom, or will their knowledge always fall so far short of the problems of the world that their history will lie always beyond their control? Is evil in the shape of discontinuity and destruction an ultimate fact, or is it somehow overruled?

The particular problems connected with special ways of asking this question must not be disregarded. Yet it is well to see that when we ask what is the status of human purpose we touch upon a larger problem underlying many special formulations. That problem is commonly called the relation between Appearance and Reality. Human purpose is an appearance. It issued from a source which it did not make and which it does not understand; likewise it will sooner or later disappear into an unknown future. What is this Reality from which our purposes emerge and into which they disappear? Is it chaos or an order?

This is an old problem and in the present Part we shall develop an old and familiar hypothesis which purports to solve it. We shall examine ideas derived from Plato and from the Old and New Testaments. Our object is not Platonic or Biblical criticism, but rather a simple search for certain general ideas which deal with our problem. After stating these ideas in their older form, we shall take time to examine the shape given them in the work of a modern professional philosopher, Alfred North Whitehead.

The central hint which we shall find and develop is that the source from which we come and into which we go is not chaos, but an order. In particular, it is the hypothesis that all things which have existed, or do exist, or will exist are governed, not by many powers, but by One Power and that this Power by making and using all things, including our plans and purposes, thereby makes sense of them. The last word therefore is not death and destruction, but somehow life beyond life.

## CHAPTER NINE

# THE SEARCH FOR PURPOSE:
# NATURE PHILOSOPHY AND
# PLATONISM

OFTEN WHEN A MAN IS BESET BY PROBLEMS OF EVERYDAY LIFE, he finds it a tonic to take a walk in the country. Similarly, when he is troubled by the thought of the mortality of human purpose and the flux of things, he may turn to the study of nature. Here he examines a record which, so far as he can ensure, is purged of human fabrication. Perhaps this record will, so to speak, return a more objective answer to his question than history. He does not ask so much for proofs as for plausible hypotheses. Having come across these, he can then try to work them up into more rigorous and adequate doctrine.

*Ends in Nature*  There are two facts, often noted, which may give him hope that flux and perishing are not final. The first is that the flux often seems to be engaged in accomplishing "ends" or purposes; the second, that throughout time and space certain familiar patterns or "laws" recur.

Suppose that he is trying to explain to a child in the simplest terms how a flower comes into existence. He starts with the seed, relating how it is blown by the wind into some crevice in the ground where a covering of earth and leaves protects it while it begins its growth. Then, he continues, rain soaks down from the surface to provide water for the germinating seed; the sun warms the ground and in time, after the snow has melted, the seed puts its first shoots above ground. Its roots go down and draw up nourishment; its leaves spread out, absorbing needed elements from the sunlight and giving off waste products. The coöperation of many things produces the full-grown plant.

At this point he catches himself and reflects on the extraordinary things he has been saying. What does he mean "coöperation?" Unlike men in community, the parts of nature do not know what they are doing. Does he mean then that there is somehow embedded within them a law or purpose which makes each perform its function and directs all parts toward a further end? Oddly, that is the hypothesis which is suggested.

For one thing, the elements in this process of making a flower do not come and immediately go. The seed sheds its husk but the embryo continues on, though in a new form. The nourishment drawn from water, soil, and air does not vanish, but takes on a new shape within the plant. Much of the perishing of things here was only apparent, not real. The old is altered, but maintained, in the new. Dewey writes: "The growth and development of any living organism from seed to maturity illustrates the meaning of continuity."[1]

Furthermore, when we look at the completed process, it seems that from the start the plant was already within the seed and other elements, not actually, of course, but potentially. These things had the power to make or become a flower. And this power was not just latent and merely possible. When we consider the elements all coming together, the flower was that which they were going to become; in other words, their purpose or end. To use Whitehead's language a little crudely, we might say that here end and elements are mutually immanent in one another.

Now, a man coming upon this suggestion may know very well that the old *Naturphilosophie* is out of favor and that many theorists ridicule the notion that there are entelechies in the world. Still solutions to these problems are not so easily come by that he can afford to dismiss without a thought this persisting impression that nature entertains ends or purposes. When he looks around him at the familiar processes of nature, he does not find simply a succession of isolated particles or moments. These particles or moments often seem to hang together. They seem to start by aiming at something, and to create in the process a single, integral thing, a whole or individual.

One finds such wholes or individuals in some of the familiar cycles of nature. In the growth of flowers and trees; in the vast, integrated life of the forest; in the round of the seasons itself where each part seems to perform a function preparing the way for the next, there is this hint of purpose, and the suggestion that destruction is not always final.

*Recurrence of patterns*   It is not likely that a man will notice this first fact, the evidence of wholes, apart from the second, the recurrence of patterns. The presence of wholes or individuals in nature shows that it is not utterly against the character of nature that there should be endurance along with change. Yet we must also see that these wholes themselves sooner or later perish. The curious fact of recurrence now suggests that even this disappearance may not be final. For one thing, while the whole or individual may in one sense perish, in another sense it does not, since its pattern may in large part reappear again and again. It disappears in actuality, but remains on in potentiality.

But what is particularly interesting, the recurrence of patterns suggests that these potentialities are a system; that they constitute one, organized potentiality or power and not many disconnected ones. For we find that nature does not do "just anything," forever creating totally new and different things, one after another. The peculiar feature of its creativity is that in its new things there are always identities with the old. That potentiality or pattern which appeared here today also appeared there many years ago and will appear elsewhere in the distant future.

Our forefathers admired, studied, and used the same kinds of trees we do. They were acquainted with mountains and plains, running rivers, flowers, the swift round of the seasons. Men in many parts of the earth and in the most distant times have known these things. Is it not a little strange that these same natures should repeat themselves in so many diverse connections and at such great distances from one another?

If nature were governed by many separate powers aiming at many different purposes, we should expect to find each of its parts quite unlike. But, instead, we find always in the differences many identities. These patterns which we trace again and again are not exclusive of one another, but are continually appearing in one another's company. Indeed, this seems to be the way nature creates, by ever-new combinations of familiar elements. Shall we say then that nature is governed not by many isolated powers, but by a single power which reaches to all its parts?

So Emerson thought. "A rule of one art, or a law of one organization," he wrote in *Nature*, "holds true throughout nature. So intimate is this Unity, that, it is easily seen, it lies under the undermost garment of nature, and betrays its source in Universal Spirit."[2] But what Emerson was particularly at pains to point out was the significance of this unity for man. Many of the patterns which recur in nature also occur in the life of man. The analogies which we trace between the various parts of nature also make them resemble parts of human history.

"What is a farm," he wrote, "but a mute gospel? The chaff and the wheat, weeds and plants, blight, rain, insects, sun— it is a sacred emblem from the first furrow of spring to the last stack which the snow of winter overtakes in the fields. But the sailor, the shepherd, the miner, the merchant, in their several resorts, have each an experience precisely parallel, and leading to the same conclusions: because all organizations are radically alike."[3]

The evidence of a purpose in the world applies to man as well as to nature. It would indicate that our purposes are

not in a fundamentally hostile world, but in one which somehow uses and treasures them along with all other created
things.

*The Hypothesis of One Power in the* Republic    If a man will
turn with our question in mind to a reading of Plato, he will
find, I think, that Plato's conclusion was something like this
conclusion. If he accepts what Plato says, he will feel that at
bottom the world is governed by a single power and that this
power is an idea. In other words, that there is one purpose
immanent in the world.

In the opening parts of the *Republic*, for instance, he will
follow an argument which is similar in form to that of the
*Naturphilosophie* which we have been developing here. The
question is the nature of Justice. But as Socrates, the principal
speaker, is careful to point out, the dialogue is not trying to
elaborate a proof, but merely to make an exposition. For
instance, Socrates argues that since the arts of the shepherd,
the pilot, the doctor, and others aim at some good for their
subjects, so must the art of governing aim at the good of the
governed. Obviously this is not a proof. Rather it is intended
to imply that since there is commonly harmony and co-
operation in the world, disharmony and oppression run counter to the fundamental tendency of things.

That fundamental tendency of things which society as
well as all nature is trying to express is rooted in the "ideas."
It is not for me to say precisely what Plato means by the
ideas. They do not comprise ideas of "mud, filth, and hair."
Neither are they confined to the mathematical forms. They
are akin to the patterns whose recurrence caught our attention
in the first part of this chapter.

The important thing to note about them here is that they
are not merely definitions or class concepts which a man might
arrive at by observing the identities in things. Neither are
they moralistic ideas which ought to be realized, but which
the world in fact may disregard. They are ends or purposes;

that is, patterns with power. They are not passive, but active. They cause things to happen in the world, not, so to speak, by forcing them from behind, but rather by being that which the things of the flux strive to become, even though they may never perfectly satisfy this striving. Being wary of the suggestion of final causes, we should prefer, like Dewey, to call them "tendencies." Yet we can hardly deny that in nature and history these "tendencies," or "real possibilities" or "probabilities," are an important part of the objective facts. In short, the facts themselves, apart from any observing mind, clearly seem to have an ideal aspect.

In the *Republic* we meet the hypothesis of One Power directly when Plato touches on the idea of good. The idea of good is the highest of the ideas. It is "that which imparts truth to the known and the power of knowing to the knower."[4] It is "not only the author of knowledge to all things known, but of their being and essence."[5] Unfortunately this conception of the good which pervades the whole dialogue and gives importance to its parts is hardly more than mentioned and is left vague and unexplained. Socrates consents to explain it only metaphorically, "for," he says, "to reach what is now in my thoughts would be an effort too great for me."[6]

This much remains unmistakably clear: that among the ideas there is a highest; that the lesser powers and purposes are not left in chaos, but are related by or in a single power. As the sun is to sight, so is the idea of good to knowledge and being. Whatever it is, it is One. It is this view which makes Plato the follower not of Heraclitus, but of Parmenides.

*The problem of necessity in Plato*   If we turn to a later dialogue, the *Timaeus*, the notion that there is one power appears as the fundamental premise of the myth of creation set out there. In the beginning, according to the narrator, Timaeus, "the father and maker of all this universe" created the world in the likeness of the eternal pattern. "Are we right," he continues, "in saying that there is one world, or that they are many and infinite? There must be one only, if the created copy is to accord with the original."[7] For, since the original pattern included all intelligible essences or ideas, so must its copy, the world, include all perceptible things. As there is one all-inclusive plan, so is there one all-inclusive realization.

But here, when we try to understand this unity of the world, we run into our great problem. For if the world is One, then, to put it simply, its parts must hang together. However, in fact, the parts of the world sometimes hang together, and sometimes do not. Along with coherence and growth, there go incoherence and destruction; along with order, disorder. In that case, the created world is not an order, but chaos.

Consider, for instance, the notable passages in the *Timaeus* concerning "necessity." After describing how the creator made the world in accord with the eternal pattern and endowed it with soul and intelligence, Timaeus turns to another side of creation, "the things which come into being through necessity." "For," he continues, "the creation is mixed, being made up of necessity and mind. Mind, the ruling power, persuaded necessity to bring the greater part of created things to perfection, and thus and after this manner in the beginning when the influence of reason got the better of necessity, the universe was created."[8]

In this passage, necessity appears as a secondary power of some kind which mind or purpose struggles with and in great measure triumphs over. The similarity of necessity to what have been called in this book "the blind forces" or "the irrationality of the world" is even more clearly seen in another passage. "The lover of intellect and knowledge," says Timaeus, "ought to explore causes of intelligent nature first of all, and, secondly, of those things which, being moved by others, are compelled to move others. And this is what we too must do. Both kinds of causes should be acknowledged by us, but a distinction should be made between those which are endowed with mind and are the workers of things fair and good, and those which are deprived of intelligence and always produce chance effects without order or design."[9]

Here in necessity or "variable cause" we have cause which is without law or intelligence. Here is a necessity "which knows no law." It is to be distinguished from that cause which aims at an end, that is, purpose. This force or thing, necessity, can be used to explain why the world fails to exemplify uniformly that order and harmony which proceeds from the orderly and harmonious creator. For here is something which is independent of the creator and the eternal pattern and which accounts for some of the facts of the world, even though mind was able to persuade it to bring the greater part of created things to perfection.

This notion of necessity could be developed until it became a principle of "matter" or "evil," independent from and opposed to the divine principle of mind. Possibly that is the construction to be put on Plato's doctrine, making it a kind of Manichaean dualism. But a world in which there are two independent forces, Good and Evil, Mind and Matter, is not a world governed by One Power, nor is it a world in which human purpose makes sense.

Here is the great difficulty of *Naturphilosophie* and the attempt to infer the existence of a single purpose from the facts as we see them. Admittedly the facts show a considerable measure of order. The supposition of a single power is not wholly out of accord with them. But it also has to be granted that this supposition does not by any means fit all the facts. As we have observed again and again, one of the common features of the world is discontinuity and destruction.

If we are going to hold that the world expresses a single purpose, then, we cannot admit that there is any real loss or destruction or discontinuity in the world's process. For if there is, then the world achieves not a single end, but more than one; it is not a universe, but a multiverse.

It is Plato's abiding conviction that there is a single purpose immanent in the world. Yet he must also record that what we often find is not unity, but plurality. He does not succeed in reconciling these two insights. For a more hopeful issue we must turn to other sources.

CHAPTER TEN

# THE STRUGGLE FOR
# EXISTENCE:
# JUDAISM AND CHRISTIANITY

FROM THE DIALOGUES OF PLATO, WE TURN TO THE OLD TESTA-
ment. From a record of the search for purpose, we turn to a
chronicle of the struggle for existence. The children of
Israel strove to survive and prosper. They wanted to acquire
great flocks and herds, beget many children, triumph over
their enemies, live to a ripe old age, and know that they
would be represented by descendants in distant generations to
come.

These are common human desires. But they were felt by
these ancient people with an uncommon intensity. Few peoples have felt as deeply as they how good it is for a man or
a race or a nation to thrive and grow strong. Few therefore
have been able to feel as deeply how dark and painful it is
that destruction should overtake men and nations. Wherever
men know the glory and terror of living they will feel a kin-
ship with these ancient prophets, fathers, sons, and lovers.

*The Promise and the Law* This is far from the mood of
Plato. Here in the Old Testament we read, not of being and
non-being, but of life and death; not of the idea of good, but
of the covenant of man and God; not of the essences or laws
of things, but of the commandments of the Lord; not of
"necessity," but of Satan, the Adversary. Yet here as in Plato
we may trace our underlying problem: Chaos or order, one
power or many?

The covenant of Iaweh and Israel is the promise that the

plans and purposes of Israel will not be in vain. In some sense, they will bear fruit and their accomplishments will be preserved. The notion of the sense in which the promise will be kept changes from time to time. One might say that it evolves as it passes from the strong, but simple, hope for progeny of the early books to the vision of a life beyond life in the Gospel. At the same time, the conception of that Power which puts the promise into effect also evolves. The hypothesis which catches our attention and stirs our hope is that the fate of the world is governed not by chance, but by One Power.

The story of the early books of the Old Testament turns around, not only the Covenant, but also the commandments of the Lord. On the one hand, there is Iaweh's promise, oft-renewed, that Israel shall prosper. On the other is the law which He has ordered Israel to keep if it would enjoy the fruits of the promise. The reader is tempted to think of the doctrine as almost a kind of tribal humanism: If Israel will abide by these rules, then it will enjoy the good things of life. If not, it will suffer pain and punishment.

One is especially struck by the utilitarian nature of the doctrine if he examines the rules and punishments which it involves. The law of sacrifice excepted, the rules and ordinances of Exodus, Leviticus, Numbers, and Deuteronomy for the most part state conditions which, according to our science of society, should have promoted the peace and strength of the Jewish nation.

Some of these rules are useful only in a few types of society. For instance, the laws of clean and unclean (Leviticus 11-16)[1] would help preserve the health of a people of that time and place, but would obviously be of little use in a modern society. Other rules have a more general application. The Ten Commandments, for instance, protect the institutions of the family, marriage, and private property. They safeguard a man in person and reputation, and establish a cult which embraces all members of the tribe and excludes all others. Most of these are conditions which promote the survival of societies now as well as then.

Likewise, the punishments are neither supernatural nor moralistic. If a man breaks the Lord's commandments, he suffers not the pangs of conscience nor the fires of hell, but rather present, worldly hurt. The wrath of the Lord takes the form of plagues, poverty, and defeat in battle, as his mercy takes the form of tangible goods and triumph. Consider, for instance, that grim warning toward the end of Leviticus which begins with these words: "But if ye will not hearken unto Me, and will not do all these commandments. . I also will do this unto you: I will appoint terror over you, even consumption and fever, that shall make the eyes to fail, and the soul to languish; and ye shall sow your seed in vain, for your enemies shall eat it" (Lev. 26:14).

Iaweh was not a deity immanent in the world. Neither was He aloof from it. If the pains and pleasures of everyday life were not actually He, they were surely His work. He spoke to certain men from the burning bush and the whirlwind. But he also spoke to common men by means of the good and ill which were their daily lot. Here there was no distinction between the laws of survival and the laws of right; between self-interest and the moral law. The commandments of the Lord recorded what was useful and practicable because His will determined what would and would not work.

*The Problem of Job*  Like ourselves the children of Israel discovered that it is not easy to get a command of the laws of social survival in their totality. The ways of the Lord, it appeared, remained mysterous even if one were acquainted with the Decalogue and the laws of Leviticus. Even if a man followed the law with the utmost fidelity, he was still liable to injury and suffering. This is the principle theme of one of the greatest of the books of the Writings, the book of Job.

Job was "whole-hearted, and upright, and one that feared God, and shunned evil." Yet evil befell Job as it should have befallen only those who had broken the commandments. His oxen and asses were stolen by raiders and his servants were slain; a fire consumed his sheep; the Chaldeans made away with his camels, and a great wind blew in the house where his sons and daughters were, and they were killed. His prosperity, his hope of offspring, and finally, with the plague of boils, the use and enjoyment of his body were taken from him.

"My face is reddened with weeping and on my eyelids is the shadow of death," complained Job, "although there is no violence in my hands, and my prayer is pure" (Job 16:16-17). He had kept the commandments. He had delivered the poor that cried, helped the fatherless, caused the widow's heart to sing for joy, and his justice was "as a robe and a diadem." Yet he now suffered the afflictions presumably reserved only for the wicked. Why?

His friends gave the conventional answers. The cause of his suffering, they repeated, lay in his own transgressions of the law. "Know therefore," said one of them, "that God exacteth of thee less than thine iniquity deserveth." However, he continued, if Job would set his heart aright and ask forgiveness, then surely the Lord would relieve him (Job 11).

Not unnaturally Job was impatient with these comfortless platitudes. They did not touch his problem. His problem was not lack of faith. He acknowledged unhesitatingly that the Lord was doing these things. He was ready to admit that he must in some manner have sinned. All he asked was to be told where and how. "Teach me," he asked, "and I will hold my peace: and cause me to understand wherein I have erred" (Job 6:24).

The conventional view was that the law and the commandments already explained what the Lord expected of man. Prosperity or suffering sprang respectively from obeying or disobeying the law. But Job's experience showed this honored formula did not hold. Sometimes the law worked and sometimes it did not. The innocent often suffer and the wicked often prosper.

Often innocence suffers and wickedness prospers: there is no question of this. And if the Lord is the Almighty, then surely this is his work. For "if it be not He, who then is it?" (Job 9:24). But if one admits this is the Lord's work, then must he not conclude that the Lord is pleased with suffering? "Is it good unto Thee," asks Job, "that Thou shouldest oppress, that Thou shouldst despise the work of Thy hands?" (Job 10:3).

It seems that if God is omnipotent, then we must say he is oppressive and unjust, while if we say he is just and that the sufferings of the innocent are not his work, then we must grant that he is not omnipotent. Job saw this dilemma many centuries before Hume stated it as a triumph of skepticism. But Job, if he did not solve it, at least refused to be discouraged by it. The Lord, he repeated in his patient, persistent way, is both almighty and just.

*Job's Problem and Ours*    The thoughts of Job are worth consulting, not for their consistency, but for their trueness to life. The conventional view, we would grant, could hardly stand up to the facts. Rewards and punishments are not equitably distributed on this earth and within the confines of history: most of us would insist on this point emphatically. Job states this proposition with poignancy. He does not make sense of it and in the end can only reiterate his faith. Yet we must note that admitting these facts undermines the original version of the Covenant and of the Lord's plan for the world.

That version was that the Israelites would obey the law, in spite of much backsliding, and that in consequence they would enjoy prosperity and increase, individually and, above all, as a nation. Here in their prosperity, and also in their deserved suffering, was the evidence that a divine purpose ruled in the affairs of men. Here was evidence that One Power governed the world, for neither hostile man nor hostile nature had the power to interfere with the realization of this plan. A single consistent law manifested itself in human history, thus making it plausible to infer that a single Power ruled over men.

Job's experience makes this version inacceptable. For now we see that sometimes lawful behavior brings prosperity and sometimes not; that sometimes, indeed, the wicked prosper while the innocent suffer. Therefore, the evidence for believing in One Power is destroyed and it becomes impossible to believe in the covenant in the old secular sense.

The problem is very like the problem which we found undermines *Naturphilosophie*. The trouble with the belief that there are particular ends in nature is that often these ends fail to materialize; the antecedents occur, but they have unexpected consequents. Likewise, the belief that there is one purpose in nature is shaken when we see how much pointless destruction goes on about us. Things come into existence and go out of existence without seeming to have any use or purpose beyond their separate existence.

Similarly, Job's problem is that in human affairs the familiar laws of the Lord (or of survival) sometimes hold and sometimes do not. The promise that lawful behavior would bring prosperity fails to be uniformly borne out by the facts. History like nature remains a problem.

If the hypothesis of One Power is to be saved, it must be radically reinterpreted. Regardless of all that can be said for it, it does not correspond to the facts as we find them. History, nature, experience, remain senseless and problematic. If we are to hold that all things are governed by a single power and that this power makes of them a saving order, a true universe, then we must hold that this order transcends history and nature. Only such a solution can solve the problem of evil and destruction with which experience confronts us. A vision of such an order and such a solution is the message of the Gospel.

*The True Importance of Purpose*  Different men will read differently the words of Our Lord and the strange story of His life and death. And they will understand differently St. Paul's incisive attempts to explain the meaning of the words and the story. It seems to me that if one will reëxamine the account of these things with the idea of this study in mind, he will find a theory which points toward a solution of our problem.

To begin with, the gospel of the kingdom is that there is another order beyond our earthly existence. Things of the world as we find it are mortal and so without consequence and meaning, except as they may be preserved in that saving order. Here the covenant with man is not that he and his children shall thrive and prosper in history. It is rather that they shall sooner or later die in history but that they shall yet live in an order which transcends history. The meek, the merciful, the pure in heart, shall inherit the earth as was promised to Abraham, but they shall inherit it, not on earth, but in heaven.

In what way then are human acts and plans important? It is clearly impossible for men to bring about with any certainty the results which their plans aim at. Regardless of our good fortune from time to time, human weakness is a fact which cannot be altered. It is senseless for you to say "today or to-morrow we will go into such a city, and continue there a year, and buy and sell, and get gain; whereas ye know not what shall be on the morrow. For what is your life? It is even a vapour, that appeareth for a little time, and then vanisheth away. For that ye ought to say, If the Lord will, we shall live, and do this, or that" (James 4:13-14).[2]

But if we cannot control the consequences of our purposes, we can at least have purposes. The important thing about a man is not so much what he accomplishes, as what he intends. In short, the important thing about him is not his success, but his soul.

Here, it hardly need be said, we have a principal theme of the Gospel. Again and again in Christ's sayings and in St. Paul's comments on them, it is repeated that what counts is

the inward character of a man, rather than his outward behavior. "Think not," He said on the Mount, "that I am come
to destroy the law, or the prophets: I am not come to destroy,
but to fulfill. . . Ye have heard that it was said by them of old
time, Thou shalt not kill; and whosoever shall kill shall be in
danger of the judgment: but I say unto you, That whosoever
is angry with his brother without a cause shall be in danger of
the judgment. . . Ye have heard that it was said by them of
old time, Thou shalt not commit adultery: But I say unto you,
That whosoever looketh on a woman to lust after her hath
committed adultery with her already in his heart" (Matt. 5: 17-
28). Again, St. Paul wrote to the Christians in Rome: "For
he is not a Jew, which is one outwardly; neither is that circumcision, which is outward in the flesh: but he is a Jew,
which is one inwardly; and circumcision is that of the heart,
in the spirit, and not in the letter" (Romans 2: 28-29).

This notion helps reconcile two ideas which often appear
in Christ's teaching and which seem to be in conflict. On
the one hand, we are adjured to do good to our fellows in this
world. We are to be merciful and to make peace; to help
the poor and feed the hungry; to love both neighbors and
enemies as ourselves. In a sense, this is a more wordly ethics
than the old law of the Levitical priesthood. For what it
holds to be important is not a ritual or sacrifice performed
solely to please the deity, but rather acts of helpfulness intended to aid other men. What pleases the deity is that we
should devote ourselves wholeheartedly to trying to improve
the world.

Yet the teaching also is that we are to disdain this world.
The saving order of things, as we have seen, is held to be not
here, where all things fail and die, but beyond. Therefore you
should "Take no thought for your life, what ye shall eat,
or what ye shall drink; nor yet for your body, what ye shall
put on. Is not the life more than meat, and the body than
raiment?" (Matt. 6: 25). And we are counseled to behold
the fowls of the air and to consider the lilies of the field

which care neither for themselves nor for one another and yet
are fed and clothed.

Now, the question which one must ask is, Which shall I
believe: That this world is important and that we should
strive to feed, clothe, and shelter one another and to care
for our worldly needs; or That this world is unimportant and
that we should largely disregard its needs and problems? When
I feed the hungry am I doing something important for them,
or is it indifferent to them whether or not they are fed? Shall
I conclude that since I should love my neighbor as myself
and since for myself I take no thought for my life or what I
eat, therefore, I need take no thought for my neighbor's life
and what he eats?

The central principle of this Christian doctrine, it seems
to me, is that by means of this other order, the kingdom of
heaven, the things of this world are spiritualized. Our purposes
must aim at bringing this present world ever closer to harmony
and perfection. Thus our purposes, as the aesthetic humanist
clearly sees, themselves gain in richness and complexity. This
is what is important to that other order: not the soul's objects
as the soul sees them, but rather the character of the soul itself.

In this way, there is a reason for having a civilized will, in
spite of the untoward consequences which often seem to flow
from such a will; there is a reason for following our best
knowledge, in spite of the fact that it seems only contingent.
The world is important as a place for the maturing of souls.

The world therefore is immensely important. It is immensely important that a man's purposes should be as inclusive
and his love as wide as he can possibly make them. He must
be intensely attached to the world, seeking continually to
deepen its harmonies. Yet at the same time he may not be
wedded to the world. He must not accept it at its face value,
on its own terms. He must also be detached from the world,
understanding that its lasting consequences are not here but
elsewhere.

He must not, let it be repeated, allow himself to be touched in the slightest by the confusion of history or the inveterate weakness of man. For if he accepts the propositions of this theory, there is nothing which can make his hope flag. No matter how much failure he sees around him or beyond him, he never gives up. For he knows that no matter what may happen here and now, all will yet be well. He will work unceasingly in this world, precisely because of his faith in the next. His motto is both Work and Peace.

*The Law of Love and Perfection*   This, it seems to me, is the heart of the doctrine: the notion that there is another order of existence and that there and there only does human purpose truly come to fruition. There are many other things to be said. One will ask, for instance, what kind of purpose he must have in order to gain entrance into this other order. Is it enough to conform to the old Levitical law or is something more required?

Christ's reply is clear, but incredible: "Be ye therefore perfect, even as your Father which is in heaven is perfect" (Matt. 5:48). We are commanded not only to love our neighbors, but also our enemies. Our only law is love and it should be a universal, all-inclusive love. It follows that we are freed from obedience to any particular code, except as it may agree with the law of love. In this sense we "have been called unto liberty" (Galatians 5:13). We are, or should be, ruled not by the law, but by the Spirit, that is, by the law of love, which in any particular case will tell us what rule to follow. We are freed from rules and codes, but only in order that we may assume a greater burden of understanding and judgment.

For it is obvious that this Christian ethics is not the clear and simple theory which, oddly, it is often held to be. Perfection, it hardly need be said, is not to be attained without hard thought and wide knowledge. How, for instance, can one both love his neighbors and his enemies? A man's enemies are those with whom his interests, and so his neighbors', come in conflict. As we have observed before, the law of love recommends that he find a reconciliation of the conflicting interests. But that may not be possible, at least for the time being. Such a reconciling interest is an invention; a product of science in the broad sense of the term, and it may happen that human science will not be equal to many of the conflicts with which it is confronted.

Likewise, freedom from a code obliges us continually to reëxamine our purposes. We must be forever searching for changes in the facts which may oblige us to alter our rule of action in order to approach as far as possible that universality of purpose which is our guiding principle. We can never remain content with a fixed personal ethics or social system, but must be always ready and anxious to alter and improve.

Above all, no man can rely on convention for his guide. So far as he can, each man must work out his own decisions. "Let every man prove his own work, and then shall he have rejoicing in himself alone, and not in another. For every man shall bear his own burden" (Galatians 6:4-5).

"The populace," wrote Emerson in *Self-Reliance*, "think that your rejection of popular standards is a rejection of all standard, and mere antinomianism; and the bold sensualist will use the name of philosophy to gild his crimes. But the law of consciousness abides. . . I have my own stern claims and perfect circle. It denies the name of duty to many offices that are called duties. But if I can discharge its debts, it enables me to dispense with the popular code. If any one imagines that this law is lax, let him keep its commandment one day."[3]

*The antinomian problem and faith* We can try to broaden our purposes. Yet it is clear from the start that our own strength can contribute only infinitesimally to that perfect order which preserves all by including all. How then can we earn the right to enter the Kingdom? The answer is, we cannot earn this right. We are saved not by good works, but by free grace. "For all have sinned, and come short of the glory of God; Being justified freely by his grace through the redemption that is in Christ Jesus" (Romans 3:23-24). Grace saves, and faith is the knowledge which a man has that he is saved.[4]

That works cannot save follows from the nature of the problem. The problem in Job's words is the impossibility "that thine own right hand can save thee." If man is saved, if there is an order of things, it is clearly not of his creation. It must be the creation, the consequence, of that One Power which rules everywhere. The problem arises because man's power is not enough. It follows that if there is a solution, it is owing to some further power.

But then, someone is sure to object, if we are saved regardless of our acts, what is the point in trying to do good and keep the law of love? Is there any need to be moral? Is there indeed any point in it?

There is point in being moral because the saving order itself is constituted by the transient orders of this world. If there is no realization and increase here, there can be none there. That order's perfection resides in the fact that it includes every other order in a single order. Without other orders, of which the harmonies of human purpose are at least one type, it could not be, let alone be perfect. In philosophical terms, Reality is composed entirely of appearances.[5]

Yet the antinomian problem remains: Why should one try to make his purposes wider if such an effort will not help earn him salvation? Suppose he has faith, the knowledge that he is saved. Why may he now not behave as wickedly and foolishly as he pleases?

The reply is to reëxamine the notion of knowledge. Knowledge, as we have seen in many connections throughout this study, is never apart from will. Our conceptions are also our plans and purposes; virtue is knowledge and knowledge is virtue. Hence, faith, the knowledge that there is One Power and that therefore you are saved, also involves the purpose of carrying out the will of that Power. That conception which makes sense of your purposes, makes sense of them as a branch of a single Power or Purpose which is being realized in all events. Therefore, if you truly believe that your purposes make sense, you will also believe you are an agent of that Power, and act accordingly. You will, as it was taught on the Mount, "let your light so shine before men, that they may see your good works." There is no antinomian problem. If you know you are saved, you will choose to do God's will.

We shall have more to say on this point later. Yet it may be noted here that if it is well taken, it follows that the *proof* of the existence of God and a *conversion* to doing His will go hand in hand. The intellectual and emotional sides of religious experience are inseparably one.

*Universalism* This is hardly an orthodox interpretation of the Gospel, although I think that in fundamentals this account and the Gospel are in harmony. However, there is one very important point on which they deeply differ. It is the question of how many are saved, all or only some.

It is possible to find certain passages which indicate that all souls will be saved. For instance, there is a passage in St. Paul's epistle to the Christians in Rome where he is describing how grace, brought into the world by Christ, has overcome death, introduced by Adam. "Therefore," he continues, "as by the offence of one judgment came upon all men to condemnation; even so by the righteousness of one the free gift came upon *all* men unto justification of life"[6] (Romans 5:18). However, one can hardly make such passages counterbalance the repeated statement, that "many are called, but few chosen."

The sense of our present theory is clearly that all are saved. The law of love which governs the world is all-inclusive. It is this which obliges us, if we would obey that law, to try to love, not only neighbors, but enemies also, including so far as we can all purposes within our own. The law is that nothing and no one will be excluded from the final order. That is why, as agents of the law, we make it our object continually to widen and deepen our circle of interests.

This view is unorthodox, but obviously it is the only way in which we can get an answer to the problem of this study. If there are in the end many created things, then there cannot be in the beginning a single purpose. If certain souls are irrevocably lost, then certain incompatibilities are final; and if certain incompatibilities are final, then all things constitute not a universe, but a multiverse. If some transient orders are left out of the final synthesis, then we have in the end not an order, but chaos.

The notion of the kingdom of heaven adds an important element to the hypothesis of One Power. It directs our attention to another order of existence which, it holds, makes sense of our present senseless experience. It thereby enables us to avoid a difficulty which troubles a man when he reads the Old Testament or Plato, viz., the impossibility of making sense of history or nature in themselves. But the doctrine of election, it seems to me, cannot stand along with the hypothesis of One Power. If one power rules and one purpose is realized, then in the end, "nothing is lost."

The notion that nothing is lost is a fundamental of philosophical idealism as it was expounded by certain writers of the last century. The Absolute Idea of Hegel is that single purpose which is being realized in all things. His Absolute Being is the single, realized consequence of that purpose which includes all partial realizations of it. This notion of a final Reality which includes and is constituted by all appearances or partial realizations is common to the work of F. H. Bradley, Josiah Royce, and Bernard Bosanquet.[7] In recent years, it has been restated, with important differences, by Alfred North Whitehead, whose ideas we shall examine in the following chapters.

## CHAPTER ELEVEN

# CREATIVE ADVANCE

WHITEHEAD'S IDEAS WILL BE EXAMINED UNDER THREE HEAD-ings.[1] We shall first look at his theory of creative advance. Here he gives a meticulous analysis of what in this essay has been called continuity. He explains how things enter into one another and how they are preserved through change. He there-fore enables us to see how human purposes may endure in spite of flux. Indeed, since this flux is creative and purposive, we also are shown how by means of flux our own purposes realize a wider purpose.

Secondly, we shall consider his theory of the soul. Ac-cording to this account, a man's soul, as his system of knowl-edge and purpose, is not an exceptional kind of thing, totally unlike things that happen in the rest of nature. The soul is another variety of the basic type of entity which constitutes the universe. Therefore, other things enter into it and it enters into other things. Knowledge is not a mere reflection of real things. Purpose is not a mere name for what might be. A man's soul is not a ghost, but a real thing, and so, in short, worth having and saving.

Also when we examine Whitehead's theory of the soul we shall see another important characteristic of some parts of the world. We shall see how a single event can happen in the body, and also in the mind or soul. Thus, we shall see how it might be possible for events to occur in human history and also to oc-cur in a further order of things which saves and uses them. Such a saving order Whitehead describes as the Consequent Nature of God.

Our third topic will be Whitehead's theory of God. We shall see how he conceives of God, on the one hand, as a single, complex purpose which reaches to all things, and, on the other, as the single created fact which is the realization of this purpose. This single created fact, the Consequent Nature of God, is not the world as we know it, but an order of existence which preserves and uses that world and all things in it, including human purpose.

This exposition, springing from Whitehead's interpretation of modern physics, throwing light upon the features of everyday experience, will, it is hoped, make the hypothesis of One Power more plausible. It should weaken some of those prejudices which make it hard to entertain this hypothesis seriously. But what of proof? Have we any positive reason for accepting this hypothesis, whether according to Whitehead's or someone else's construction of it? This question and the conclusions to be drawn from our whole account, will occupy the last sections of this Part.

*The Theory of Mutual Immanence*   The fundamental principles of the theories of knowledge and morals sketched in this essay agree with Whitehead's ideas. That these principles were worked out largely in the course of an examination of Dewey's ideas should not be surprising. The two men, while they disagree on "last things," agree profundly on their analysis of experience and process, as Dewey has indicated in certain comments on Whitehead's philosophy.[2]

Some of the words used in the exposition in previous parts of this essay were taken from Whitehead's usage. For the most part, however, the argument was stated in everyday language. In order to make the exposition more exact, as well as more faithful to Whitehead, we must now use the unfamiliar words of his own statement. These words, while unfamiliar, are clearly defined and consistently used by him and they have the immense advance of shaking off confusions which cling inevitably to many of the terms used in traditional controversy.

The heart of Whitehead's theory of creative advance is the notion of mutual immanence. The parts of the world enter into one another. When we analyze the present we find within it elements of both the past and the future. These parts, "the final real things of which the world is made up" he calls *actual entities*. What is an actual entity? God is an actual entity. So also are the members of that "stream of electrical occasions" which physics finds at the base of natural objects. But the simplest way to begin the definition of an actual entity is to mention the particular acts which make up anyone's everyday experience. To jump out of bed; to say "Hello" to someone; to light a cigarette; to drive to work, each of these is an actual entity or a closely related group of actual entities. To be more precise would be to explain the theory of creative advance. With Whitehead's theory as with an actual entity, you cannot properly say the first thing about it until you have already said the last.

An actual entity is a compounding of other actual entities. An actual entity is primarily composed of its past. When you analyze it into its parts, you find those actual entities which gave rise to it.

You know this because, for instance, you find that the actual entity has the properties of other actual entities in its past. For the purposes which concern these properties, it is indifferent whether you use this actual entity or whether you use one in its more or less recent past. This fact is a matter of common sense. You know that your friend continues to display his peculiar and engaging qualities. He is much the same friend today as he was yesterday or a year ago. In greater or less degree, the same is true of most of the familiar objects of our everyday occupations.

This past which primarily produces and constitutes an actual entity, Whitehead calls a *nexus*. It is not itself the actual entity; it is equivalent to Dewey's "means." Hence, to analyze an actual entity into the elements of its nexus is the same as to analyze a consequence into its means.

When an actual entity enters into the constitution of another actual entity, it is spoken of as a *physical prehension* and the second actual entity is said to *prehend* the first. In entering into another actual entity, the first is united with the other actual entities constituting this second actual entity. Hence, it is only a part of the second actual entity. The prehension of the first by the second therefore is the first actual entity entering into the second in a certain manner or mode, which manner is one aspect of the character of the second actual entity.

When one analyzes an actual entity he divides it into physical prehensions. These prehensions, on the one hand, take him back to the actual entities constituting the present actual entity and, on the other, they reveal the various manners in which the past entities enter into the present one and thereby contribute to its character.

An actual entity comprises many physical prehensions, yet it is itself a unity. The prehending of the actual entities of the nexus is a *concrescence*, a "growing together", of these actual entities in these various modes. To explain in terms of conscious experience: You know that there is one entity here because in further experience you find this group or nexus of actual entities acting together as one. The group has the effect not of a multiplicity of actual entities, but of one. Of course, precisely what effect the actual entity will have will depend upon the context of that further experience. One actual entity can enter differently into different further stages of experience. However, this does not mean that the further stage of experience makes the unity of the actual entity. The prehensions are already unified; that is why they register as a unity in the later stage. The later stage of experience, we might say, "interprets" them.

We can relate this notion to our previous discussion. A concrescence is comparable to what Dewey calls the solving of a problem. As a man solves new problems in his pursuit of old ends, his system of knowledge and purpose will be reinterpreted. He cannot say what his perspective is until by problem-solving he has made some addition to it, and so provided himself with a ground for interpreting it. It follows that what interpretation he gains of his perspective depends upon the kind of knowledge which he adds to his system. Perspective is a curious thing. For it is that in terms of which a man interprets the facts; yet all he ever sees of it is one among many possible interpretations.

Perspective, as the system of knowledge and purpose of a conscious being, is a peculiarly complex actual entity, as we shall see shortly. However, the characteristic which we are discussing here applies to actual entities of all kinds. This characteristic is that an actual entity has many possible ways in which it may enter into other actual entities. It may be prehended by other actual entities in any one of a number of possible manners. Hence, in this sense, the actual entity is defined by the concrescence in which it makes a further actual entity.

That concrescence which made the first actual entity is fixed and unalterable; it is "stubborn fact." Yet at the same time, it is always open to "reinterpretation." On the one hand, the concrescence constitutes one complex, fully determinate "atom." But this atom is anything but irreducible or inert. It does things; it works; it has power. And what it does expresses its own nature or potentiality.

*The principles of Process and Relativity*   There are two notions which are particularly important. The first is that an actual entity is precisely the way the actual entities of its nexus come together; it is their unified mode of becoming. We have spoken of the actual entities of the nexus as "constituting" the further actual entity. But it must not be thought that the process of becoming is separate from the product. The product is nothing more than the process. "*How* an actual entity *becomes*," writes Whitehead, "constitutes *what* that actual entity *is*; so that the two descriptions of an actual entity are not independent. Its 'being' is constituted by its 'becoming.' This is the 'principle of process.' "[3]

Experience grows in buds or drops, the actual entities. These actual entities in turn become and do work. When we look at what they are doing, we refer to the previous actual entities as "they" or "it." We say that "they" or "it" does so-and-so. And we fall into the habit of thinking of the world as composed of more or less fixed things or "subjects" which also manage somehow to do things. Our habits of speech, built around the distinction between the subject which "is" and the predicate which "does" or "inheres," encourage this way of thinking.

This is a convenient habit, enabling us to concentrate on certain aspects of things and lump the others together as the "thing" or "subject" doing them. But it is not an accurate analysis of experience or nature. For if we will examine these "subjects" we shall find them in process too. All process, as well as that variety of it we call experience, grows in buds. But it is also a fact that each bud enters into a process which constitutes a further bud. Hence, in analyzing nature and experience, we never find that which becomes but which is not itself a becoming.

Whitehead expresses the principle of process as a conclusion of physics: "The physical things which we term stars, planets, lumps of matter, molecules, electrons, protons, quanta of energy, are each to be conceived as modifications of conditions within space-time, extending throughout its whole range. There is a focal region, which in common speech is where the thing is. But its influence streams away from it with finite velocity throughout the utmost recesses of space and time . . . For physics the thing itself is what it does, and what it does is this divergent stream of influence."[4]

It is impossible to explain the principle of process without also touching the principle of relativity. For in saying that *what* an actual entity is, is the *manner* in which its constituents become, we are also saying that the constituents are not only themselves but also the actual entity which they produce. To state the point simply, but generally, we can say that every actual entity has the power to enter into a further becoming or concrescence. This is the nub of the principle of relativity.

It should not be hard for the social scientist to grant that the principles of process and relativity apply to his subject matter. The "objects" which he deals with are normally the processes of society, of institutions, of individual men. When, for instance, the student of politics describes Congress, he states how Congressmen are elected, how Congress behaves, how its acts affect the country. For him Congress is the Federal legislative process.

In describing the passage of some bill, he will note the social changes in which the demand for it originated; the pressures which brought this demand to Congressional attention; the procedures, formal and informal, by which the demand became law. He will note that the passage of the bill is accomplished in various stages and that the single process of its origination and enactment can be broken down into constituent processes. He will show how the earlier stages enter actively and constitutively into the later stages of process; how, for example, the manner in which the House committee hearings on the bill affect the manner in which the House votes. He will not be content with describing each of these constituent processes "in itself," but will describe them in relation to one another, showing how each functions in the process as a whole. Throughout he will be concerned with events, happenings, process, rather than inert things and will describe each element in its relations with the environing whole.

*Potentiality: the conceptual pole*   One actual entity will enter into the concrescence which constitutes a further actual entity and the way the first actual entity functions, the mode of its prehension, will express something of its own nature or potentiality. The actual entity is fully determinate and one, but it also has the power to function and have effects in further stages of process. This is stating the facts very roughly. We must now analyze more carefully this notion of potentiality. Every actual entity is the real togetherness of the actual entities of its past. But this could not be so unless actual entities had the power of functioning in the concrescence of further actual entities. That applies to the present actual entity as well as to those of its past. Hence, we cannot describe an actual entity solely by referring to its past, but must also say something about "the element of futurity" in it, its potentiality.

In every actual entity then there are two aspects or poles. On the one hand, there are the physical prehensions which are the coming together of the actual entities of its nexus. On the other hand, there is the power of this unified set of prehensions to do further work. This second aspect of an actual entity Whitehead calls its "conceptual" or "mental" pole.

These are not very apt names. They suggest consciousness, while this second aspect of an actual entity only rarely involves consciousness. Perhaps "potential" pole would be a better name. A any rate we can try to remember the reason for looking for a name; viz., the fact that it is a characteristic of actual entities that they can enter into and constitute further actual entities.

Whitehead goes on from this fact to reinterpret the Platonic notion of a realm of ideas. The conceptual pole, according to his account, is composed of conceptual prehensions. In this kind of prehension there is prehended not an actual entity, but rather an *eternal object*. An eternal object is not what common sense calls a thing, but rather a pattern or form. It is Whitehead's term for the Platonic "ideas." For instance, it refers to those familiar, recurring patterns of everyday experience which we noted in Chapter IX. But it refers to them, not as patterns characterizing facts of the world, but rather as *possibilities* of what fact may be. Whitehead calls them "pure potentials for the specific determination of fact," and "forms of definiteness."

When an eternal object is conceptually prehended, it is

part of the potentiality of the actual entity which has these conceptual prehensions. When this actual entity is physically prehended in a further concrescence, the manner in which it is prehended expresses its potentiality. This manner, or *subjective form*, of the physical prehension may be called the "physical embodiment" of the eternal object prehended conceptually by the previous actual entity.

It must not be thought that this physical embodiment is more like everyday experience, or more real than the conceptual prehension. The central principle of this account of process is that everyday experience unites inextricably both kinds of embodiment or prehension. Therefore, a man's perception of a pattern—his glance at a tree, his sight of a familiar face—involves both a physical and a conceptual side. On the one hand, that perception is something "given," something which he feels directly and, so to speak, simply has within him. On the other hand, that perception is also purposive, involving further action on his part, as when, for instance, the tree is a landmark showing the way to some place, or a familiar face stimulates a greeting.

An actual entity has both poles, both kinds of prehension. The side of the physical prehensions is no more "actual" than the side of the conceptual prehensions. Actuality, the world, everyday experience—however you care to refer to the fundamental traits of things in nature and experience—exhibits the union of elements of both past and future. This is the notion of mutual immanence.

There is much in this account which Dewey could accept. In the means-consequence relation, the means and the consequence are mutually immanent. The means become the consequence; the consequence is the becoming of the means. Yet we can imagine Dewey's horror at the use of the term "eternal object" and the attempt to take seriously Plato's realm of ideas. However, it must be noted, Dewey's analysis of experience illuminates and illustrates that aspect of process which obliges one to grant that there is in some sense a "conceptual pole."

Dewey is not a positivist; that is, he will not confine experience to the "given," to the clearly observed facts. He shows how "tendency," the emergence of some future state of fact, characterizes any present state of fact. His analysis reflects faithfully the obvious sense of everyday experience, that any given situation is shot through with possibilities which are intrinsic to the facts of the situation. This sense of movement toward the future is the source of that contrast between the stable and the precarious which is a fundamental characteristic of human experience and which is the theme of a magnificent opening chapter in *Experience and Nature*.

*Feeling as Positive Prehension*   Mutual immanence can be further explained with the help of another term which Whitehead often uses instead of "prehension." When prehensions, physical or conceptual, are positive they are also called *feelings*. Negative prehensions are of crucial importance to this theory, but for the sake of exposition we shall consider at present only those prehensions which can also be called feelings. Also it should be noted that the feeling which is referred to only rarely involves consciousness. In the generic sense in which the word is used here, the electronic occasions of physics, as well as the moments of conscious experience, feel one another.

Nevertheless, the sense of the word and so of prehension can be illustrated from conscious experience. Roughly, there are two kinds of conscious feelings. A man may say, "I feel the heat." What he is getting at here is that something is happening to him; the heat is entering into him. He feels hot; that is, he *is* hot. Here emphasis is upon feeling or prehension in its physical mode. What he feels is something simply *given* to him and *had* by him.

On the other hand, he may also say, "I feel angry." What he is getting at here is that something is welling up within him; he is about to do or say something antagonistic to the person or thing arousing his anger. He feels that action coming into existence. Here emphasis is upon feeling or prehension in its conceptual mode.

These examples may be used to get a clearer notion of what prehension involves. But it must not be thought that they are pure cases respectively of physical and conceptual prehension. There are no such pure cases to be found, in experience or in nature. As we observed above, any feeling which a man has, such as a perception, joins both sorts of basic prehension or feeling. We shall turn to the analysis of these more complex feelings, the "intellectual" feelings, in the next chapter. But it must be emphasized here that even in the case of unconscious process, the two sorts of prehension are also inseparably joined together. Any actual entity is composed of both physical and conceptual prehensions.

To generalize the point: Knowledge is also purpose because each physical prehension is united with a corresponding conceptual prehension. Merely knowing a thing, the receiving of it into experience, involves willing it, the projecting of that thing into the future. What a man has known in the past helps determine what he will look for in the future: the class or national background of his thought will determine his perspective. What he has been in the past helps determine what he will be in the future: habits developed in the past will set the line of conduct by which he explores the future. What has been and what has been known does not wholly determine the future, for process is creative. But the reproduction of the past is an important part of the future—where there is continuity.

*Reproduction* We have emphasized that prehension of the conceptual pole which prehends the newly ingressing eternal object. There is another aspect of the potentiality of an actual entity. An actual entity not only has the power to "reproduce" itself in the concrescence of another actual entity; it also has the power to "reproduce" any and all of its constituent actual

entities. Suppose we start from a set of actual entities which
is the nexus for an emergent actual entity. When this emergent
actual entity itself functions in a further concresence it will
be a member of a nexus which also includes that set of actual
entities from which we started.

The nexus of a concrescence includes not only the actual
entities of its "recent" past, but also the actual entities which
constituted the nexūs (plural) of those actual entities in the
recent and distant past. Each concrescence is the coming together of all the actual entities of its recent and its distant past.

This fact is "reflected" in the newly ingressing eternal object. That eternal object has a unique quality which gives it
unity. Yet it is also complex, being composed of constituent
eternal objects. These constituent eternal objects are identical
with the eternal objects which ingressed into the concrescences
of all the actual entities of the emerging actual entity's past.
There should be no difficulty with this point. It simply states
in the mode of potentiality what has been said in the previous
paragraphs. That is, the complex eternal object prehended by
the conceptual pole of an actual entity is the power of that
actual entity to function in further concrescences and of that
actual entity's constituents to function in further concrescences.

This power of "reproduction" is familiar. An act which
at one time is seen in connection with certain consequences,
at another time is seen to have further and different consequences. Since an important fact about any act or event is
its consequences, it follows that in a sense the act itself is
altered by later history. Its stream of consequences fluctuates
and we as observers see it "in the light of different consequences." Hence, as we noted before, the act in one sense is
fixed and unalterable and in another sense, since it does work
in the future, it is continually "reinterpreted" by these further
consequences.

Time is irreversible, but history, both as the stream of
events and as our record of them, is never finished. For this

reason, the present and future, so to speak, have the past at their mercy. For here in the present and future the consequences of the past are creatively drawn out. Here occur those later events "in the light of" which earlier events prove to be injurious or beneficial, and men of another age far-sighted or ridiculous, champions of progress or of reaction.

*Final Causation*    The notion of a conceptual pole refers to the fact that an actual entity can enter into and function in the becoming of a further actual entity. The peculiar fact is this: that an actual entity is the coming together of many actual entities, yet when it functions in a further concrescence, it functions not as many, but as one. We call it *an* actual entity precisely for this reason: namely, that it can be felt or prehended as a single entity by a further actual entity.

We say the actual entity *is* a unity before it has been felt or prehended. It is prehended as a unity only because it already is a unity. As we mentioned before, in terms of experience, we know that the many actual entities of the nexus have created a single entity, a bud of experience, because we feel or perceive them as a unity in a later stage of experience.

Before it was felt, the actual entity was not a unity in the sense of being physically a unity. It was a unity in the sense of being potentially a unity. However, this is no depreciation of its singleness. As we have seen, potentiality is one of the important ways things can be something—one of the basic modes of being. The conceptual side of an entity then is the unification of an entity in the mode of potentiality.

This conceptual unity of an actual entity must not be thought of as something, so to speak, tacked on in the later stages of the concrescence. This unity has affected the concrescence from its earliest stages. Each of the actual entities of the nexus, it will be recalled, is physically prehended in a certain manner. But it must be emphasized that this prehension in one only of many possible manners is not a distortion of the actual entity, but an "interpretation." The actual entity of the nexus is really there in the becoming of the present actual entity. However, it is there in a certain connection, namely, the company of the other actual entities of the nexus. The actual entity is there in a certain manner, and this manner is the manner of togetherness or unity of the whole set of actual entities of the nexus.

Hence, already in the physical prehensions making up the actual entity, the conceptual unity of the actual entity is having effect. For the manner of togetherness of the actual entities of the nexus is, of course, the unity of the emerging actual entity. It is this manner which will be felt by further concrescences. As we have seen, this unity should be called conceptual. But that does not mean it is separate from what it unifies. On the contrary, the unifying conceptual prehension pervades the concrescence from its earliest stages. So, on the one hand, the concrescence, since it is made by its constituents, is a process of efficient causation. On the other hand, since the unifying conceptual prehension pervades the concrescence from the start, it is a process of final causation. There is mutual interaction between the emerging whole and its parts. Cause and effect, means and consequence, past and present, present and future, are mutually immanent.

In this theory of final causation, we have what remains of the notion that there are "ends" in nature. In our discussion of *Naturphilosophie* we saw that one might hold, as presumably ancient and medieval thinkers did, that there is a set of patterns which the flux continually seeks to realize. It must be emphasized with all possible force that Whitehead's theory of final causation utterly rejects the notion that the number of "forms" or "ends" is limited or that nature or history is essentially repetitious, trying always with only greater or less success to realize the same finite set of forms. Whitehead's view on the contrary, is not a theory of a repetitious or cyclical world, but a theory of creative advance. Process is creative precisely because the "ends" which emerge are not repetitions, but genuinely novel.

*Summary*   Whithead's terms may seem strange at first, yet the theory of mutual immanence conforms remarkably well with the outlines of ordinary experience. There are no inert and stable things; everything is in constant motion and what a thing is is how it acts. Sugar is sweet, that is, it sweetens. The Senator is a Democrat, that is, he votes Democratic. How a thing acts depends not only on itself, but also on the environment in which it operates. A chemist by appropriate combinations can elicit other properties than sweetness from sugar. A crisis may bring to light other potentialities of the Senator than his Democracy. Events of the past do not simply vanish; they leave "traces" which vitally affect the behavior of things of the present. Events of the future do not suddenly come upon us; they emerge from the facts of the present and are shadowed forth in the "tendencies" of these facts.

So far the theory of mutual immanence makes easy, good sense. But there is a difficulty raised by these notions of "traces" and "tendencies" which must be faced. If we are to take the theory of mutual immanence seriously, we may not think of these "traces" as a mere mark or deposit left on the present by a past which has gone out of existence. We must see them as evidence pointing to the larger fact that past events are "really together" with present events. Similarly, we must understand that the "tendencies" of present fact are not separate and different from the entity emerging from the present situation. They are that entity as it affects the present moment of process. In short, we must grant that events, which in one sense are separate in time as past, present, and future, in another sense occur  simultaneously and in the same "present."

Our more analytical notions incline us to think of the parts of time as marked off into lengths such as seconds or minutes. It follows that the process of one moment cannot be really together with the process of another. Here our "learned knife" of analysis has separated what in living fact is not separate. For if we will set aside our analytical prejudice for a moment and look at the actual processes of nature or experience, we shall see that time is not only analytical, but also synthetic, i.e., continuous. What is the "present" is defined by an event, or, in Dewey's terms, the solution of a problem. That event or solution may be "short" or "long" by the clock. But within it the whole and its constituents are mutually immanent. Analysis will break down the event into operations which themselves constitute a "present" within which subsidiary operations can be discerned. On the other hand, synthesis will show the event to be part of a larger event or problem which defines a still more inclusive present.

Consider a simple example. When a man shifts the gears of an automobile, it normally takes him only a moment. He does not concentrate on shifting from first to second; then on shifting from second to high. It is one, continuous operation, performed all at once in a single "present." Of course, this single operation consists of included operations. Yet as he performs one of the included operations, for example, shifting from first to second, that operation is not self-contained and separate, but is modified by the operation of shifting from second to high. As he performs the first operation, he is already allowing for and preparing for the next operation. The manner in which he will perform the next operation is already affecting the manner in which he performs the first. Likewise, the way he performs the first will affect the second. And throughout, the necessity of performing all operations in a smooth and successful movement will have been affecting the way the constituent operations are performed. Emerging whole and constituent parts reciprocally affect one another.

For anyone with normal skill and luck, this operation of shifting gears is only a subsidiary operation in a more inclusive process of driving a car. And that operation in turn may be for the driver a means to a further end, such as getting to work. Each operation or stage of process constitutes a "present" which analysis may break up into constitutent "presents," but only at the risk of losing sight of the more inclusive unity.

At any second in the day, you are concerned with problems on many different "levels." There is an immediate problem on which your attention is sharply focused. That problem itself is a step to the solution of a more inclusive problem. As you analyze your experience, you find these more immediate problems indicating the outlines of more and more inclusive events which you are working out. From the small business of starting cars or writing letters you pass to the larger business of raising a family or pursuing a career or "finding yourself." Similarly, an event of society or nature occurs in an environment or "field" or nexus of a more inclusive event; and that event in turn is part of the nexus of a still wider event; and so on. Each part is sensitive to, is prehended by, the larger unities which it is making and is made by.

On the one hand, process is discrete: it is composed of actual entities or operations which are atomic. Thinking of this aspect, we represent time under some image such as a linear succession of dots. But process is also continuous. If we must have an image under which to think of this aspect of time, we may think of an expanding point of light.

Discreteness and continuity are not incompatible. Whitehead's analysis of concrescence shows how both are fundamental characteristics of process. The actual entity of a nexus is not lost. It remains on actively and is used in the concrescence of that nexus. It contributes to the creation of the actual entity of that nexus. At each stage there is enrichment, development, growth, as eternal objects, hitherto unrealized, ingress into actuality. A concrescence is a process of creative continuity.[5]

In many processes there is continuity. In analyzing such processes we find mutual immanence. We find efficient causation, that is, the constituents entering into and determining the whole. We also find final causation, that is, the whole determining the manner in which the constituents will be felt. And we find the whole process of mutual interaction defining a single present. Such moments of process are, so to speak, models of that Saving Order which includes all processes of all time in a single timeless present.[6]

If all experience were like this, there would be no problem of purpose. The history of a man or a society would be a triumphal process to ever greater knowledge and power, an unending success story. But there is another trait of experience which to common sense seems as basic as continuity. Experience is also, not merely discrete, but discontinuous, frustrating, painful, haunted by failure and death. In many processes we do not find mutual immanence. We may find some "traces" of the past, but much has been lost. We find "tendencies" toward the future, but these tendencies may be frustrated and the potentialities they stand for may not be realized. Here in discontinuity is the fact which raises the problem of purpose. In the next chapter we shall consider that problem in terms of Whitehead's analysis and state a solution which his analysis suggests.

## CHAPTER TWELVE

# A SAVING ORDER

THE PROBLEM OF PURPOSE IS A FEELING WHICH OCCURS IN A special type of actual entity which we may call a soul, or mind, or personality. In this chapter we shall approach the problem of purpose through Whitehead's theory of the soul.

*Soul and Body*   There is no such thing as "the" soul if by that you mean a subject or substance enduring unaltered through a man's life-history. There is a process of thinking and feeling and, if we call this process the soul, we must remember that like all process it is composed of those atoms of becoming called actual entities. "The ancient doctrine that 'no one crosses the same river twice,'" writes Whitehead, "is extended. No thinker thinks twice; and, to put the matter more generally, no subject experiences twice."[1]

But this flux, it must be noted, is very different from the Heraclitan river. Where experience is continuous its parts do not appear only to vanish. On the contrary, they remain on actively in later stages. It is never the same river twice, so to speak, not because its waves pass and disappear, but rather because it is a sea which is filling up.

This capacity of the past to carry over into the present is not by any means confined to happenings in the mind. It is a fundamental characteristic of everything everywhere, of all actual entities. For this reason, one may say that Whitehead has taken the characteristics usually attributed to mind alone and shown that they apply to nature as well. There is no inert matter anywhere; there are no wholly discrete and separate particles of anything. So far as concerns this basic characteristic, which centers around the fact of feeling or prehension,

Whitehead finds that nature has fundamentally the same character as mind.

Likewise, mind has fundamentally the same character as nature. Actual entities, as we have seen, are not mere reflections of their constituents; they are their constituents. So what a man sees, remembers, feels, is not only "outside" him, but also "inside" him; it constitutes his mind or soul. When you look about you and perceive the color and a noise of the world; its sadness and excitement, its incredible richness in men and events, all this is yourself. Lines of process from the environment; impulses originating largely in the organism; above all, a rich inheritance of influence from your own mental past, these streams of actuality come together in every moment of your thought and feeling.

This is anything but subjectivism. The whole burden of this doctrine is to show that there is sense in our belief in an external world. We must not think of the mind or soul as something ghostly and cut off from the body and nature. The soul emerges from nature. A phrase from theology enables us to emphasize this point, although with some exaggeration: in the soul there is a resurrection of the body.

However, compared with most actual entities which we are acquainted with, the soul is enormously rich in its connections with a wide past. In the soul the comparatively simple actual entities occurring in the body and nature are transformed creatively into an actual entity of great depth and complexity.

"In a living body of a high type," writes Whitehead, "there are grades of occasions [actual entities] so coördinated by their paths of inheritance through the body, that a peculiar richness of inheritance is enjoyed by various occasions in some parts of the body. Finally, the brain is coördinated so that a peculiar richness is enjoyed now by this and now by that part; and thus there is produced the presiding personality at that moment in the body."[2]

He has put the same point more succinctly in another place.

"The human body," he writes in *Adventures of Ideas*, "is an instrument for the production of art in the life of the human soul."[3]

There is no need to exaggerate the measure of coördination which the soul gives the body. As Whitehead notes, there seem to be many actions of the body which are not governed by a unifying directive agent, and whose influence touches the soul little, if at all. However, the richness of the soul arises in important part from the fact that it is the real togetherness of many of the processes of the body.

This introduces an important fact. The soul inherits from the body, but at the same time the processes of the body inherit from one another. Hence, an actual entity in such a bodily process has two (if not more) futures, one in the soul and another in the body. Such an actual entity will function in two different continua of process. To put it crudely, it will be in two places at the same time.

To say that an actual entity can function in two different continua of process sounds odd, yet it is not hard to illustrate from common experience. Suppose two people hear a speech. There is the speech "in itself"—*the* thing which both people heard. Yet we cannot separate the speech from its consequences. And we find that it has two sets of consequences, one in the mental history of each of the listeners. The speech is functioning in two different continua of process; it is in two different "places" at the same "time."

The case is similar with the soul and the actual entities which it prehends. All parts of the body and the body's environment are in process, but certain parts maintain themselves with greater stability and identity by inheritance from their pasts. Yet the actual entities composing these lines of process may also be prehended by the soul. That is why our knowledge is "objective"; the "objects" of knowledge really enter into the soul. There are actual entities which function in the future of the body or its environment and at the same time in the soul.

Processes in the body and environment affect the soul. In turn the processes of the soul affect the body and through the body the surrounding environment. In this way the purposes of the soul are carried out.

Any particular action of the body rarely shows the whole purpose of the soul at that moment. When, for instance, a man decides to walk across the room and pick up a book, this purpose, which forms in one instance of his experience, is expressed by his bodily actions in a series and in actions of different parts of his body. The *wholeness* of his purpose is revealed by no single one of these acts, but must be reconstructed by the observer from his observation of them separately.

The soul must remain something of a mystery to the outside observer, for he can never perceive its wholeness, but only infer it, and that with very inadequate evidence. For a man's purpose rarely remains the same throughout all the acts which he originally settled upon. He is continually readjusting that purpose in the light of facts turned up by his progress. Hence, the historian of his bodily motions gets but a poor record of the seething, complex processes which are peculiarly the man himself.

One is reminded of those motion pictures which try to portray the creation of a poem or picture or other work of art. In truth, most of such creation goes on in the artist's mind. If you look at him from the outside it is a dull sight. He may be scratching himself, diddling with a pencil, or just staring vacantly into space. For a motion picture this will not do. So the artist is made to clasp his forehead, beat his breast, look heroic, all of which is neither art nor life.

The social scientist must take the soul seriously. There is a temptation to describe what a man or group is by confining yourself to recording what the man or the group does. This method is proper for the study of "natural fact." Nature has a certain transparency, revealing what it is in what it does. But man is natural fact, and something more. He has an "inside" as well as an "ouside." If the social scientist would get at the important facts about a man, he must not only observe him carefully but also make some inference about the state of his soul. There is no operational substitute for imaginative insight.

*Creativity of the Soul*  In fundamentals the creativity of the soul is no different from creativity elsewhere. The actual entity which is the presiding personality at any moment prehends a mental past of previous experience. Actual entities originating in body and environment concresce with the personality in the course of experience. In this way a man learns, the personality grows, the soul is enriched.

As an organization of its physical prehensions, the personality is a system of knowledge. It *has* the past in the shape of organized memory. As an organization of conceptual prehensions, it is a system of purpose. Its conceptual pole includes those eternal objects which have ingressed in its constituent actual entities. Furthermore, its conceptual pole prehends that complex eternal object which unifies these constituent eternal objects. This unifying eternal object is a new ingression into actuality and is the peculiarly creative aspect of the personality in that moment.

The conceptual feeling which prehends the unifying eternal object is the perspective of the personality. What actual entities will concresce with the personality in the future will be a function of this perspective. Actual entities exhibiting eternal objects already exemplified in the past of the personality will concresce with the personality. That is, in inquiry, the mind will readily identify familiar facts. However, actual entities defined by eternal objects not exemplified in the past of the personality may or may not concresce with the personality. That is, the mind may or may not perceive new aspects of facts. Whether such an actual entity will concresce with the personality depends on the *relevance* of its unifying eternal object to the eternal object defining the perspective of the personality. This refers to a familiar fact of inquiry. The inquiring mind is not bound by its perspective to perceive only that type of fact which it has already perceived. The inquiring mind can learn; it can perceive new facts. But not just any facts. The new facts it perceives must have a relevance to what it knows. Generalizations drawn from past experience are the means by which we interpret new experience and by which in the course of interpretation we extend creatively those generalizations.

By reflective thought, in other words, by rehearsal of past experience by means of symbols, and by tentative experiment, the mind develops creative hypotheses. Such a creative hypothesis is the unifying conceptual prehension of the presiding personality of the moment. It is not only a reflection of the past, for example, a generalization expressing the statistical probabilities of the environment felt by the mind in the past. Such a hypothesis, as Dewey's account emphasizes, is creative; it goes beyond the past. There is in such a creative hypothesis a nonstatistical judgment of probability. There is what Whitehead calls "an intuition of intrinsic suitability of some definite outcome from a presupposed situation," and "an intuition of probability respecting the origination of some novelty."[4] The solution of a problem, in short, is not mechanical, consisting merely in applying rules and analogies to the given facts. It is also creative, involving insight.

*Consciousness*    The characteristics of the soul which we have so far considered set it off from other types of process as differences of degree. Mental process is far richer and more complex and more creative than other processes with which we are acquainted. There is a further distinguishing characteristic of the soul: consciousness.

Whitehead uses the term consciousness in a rather narrow sense. If we take feeling to be the peculiar characteristic of mind, then we need search no farther for a way to distinguish mind from nature. Such a conclusion is not open to Whitehead, and he finds that special mark of consciousness and hence of mind in a certain class of feelings which he calls the intellectual feelings.

The intellectual feelings arise from the integration of conceptual feelings and physical feelings. We are interested only in one aspect of the theory of these feelings and so shall trace their origin only briefly. We start from the fact that in each act of becoming there are, on the one hand, physical prehensions and, on the other, conceptual prehensions derived from them, directly, where there is reproduction, and indirectly, where there is creation.

There may also arise in the course of the concrescence a further kind of prehension which Whitehead calls a *propositional feeling*. A propositional feeling is the integration of a conceptual feeling with the physical feeling from which it was derived. As physical feelings are really together in a concrescence, so may conceptual and physical feelings be really together in a propositional feeling. In such a feeling the eternal object prehended conceptually is felt not simply as a possibility, but as a *real possibility* of some subordinate nexus within the nexus of the concrescence. This subordinate nexus constitutes the "logical subjects" of the proposition, but they are felt not as an actual entity with such-and-such characteristics but simply as "it," as a something to which this real possibility is attached.

For instance, when a man is in the process of problem-solving as Dewey describes it, he runs over in his mind various possible lines of action. But these are not thought of as mere possibilities, as something which in general can be done by man or nature, but rather as something which can be done here and now. They do not individually solve the problem. A man must work through various possibilities, rejecting some, putting others together, until he finally has the plan provided by his "most probable knowledge." The propositional feelings are "lures for feeling." That is, they suggest ways toward a solution of the problem.

In this explanation it was necessary to refer to conscious experience, but the propositional feelings according to Whitehead are not conscious fellings. An *intellectual*, i.e., *conscious*, *feeling* arises from a further integration in which a propositional feeling is joined with a physical feeling. In the simplest case, this physical feeling is of the same nexus as that from which the conceptual feeling was derived. Hence, we have a feeling of a real possibility being integrated with the "physical embodiment" of that possibility. Here there is a contrast between what really might be (but which also might not be) and what actually is. This contrast between real possibility and sheer fact is the distinctive mark of conscious feelings and so of mind or soul.

"Consciousness," writes Whitehead, "is the subjective form involved in feeling the contrast between the 'theory' which *may* be erroneous and the fact which is 'given.' "[5] And again: "Consciousness requires more than the mere entertainment of theory. It is the feeling of the contrast of theory, as *mere* theory, with fact, as *mere* fact. This contrast holds whether or no the theory be corect."[6]

On the one hand there is stubborn fact; on the other hand there is something inseparable from stubborn fact. This other side is immensely important for fact, since it is that which directs and governs fact. And yet it is also tentative and hypothetical. Consciousness is the feeling of this contrast.

A similar view of consciousness emerges from Dewey's ideas. On the one hand, the problem-solver feels the novel, problematic future emerging; on the other, he tries to see what it is going to be. He examines the given facts in order to see what augury they yield. They tell him what similar facts have produced in the past. They do not suggest mere possibilities, but real possibilities. Yet this knowledge remains hypothetical. It may or may not be borne out by the facts. According to Dewey, consciousness is peculiarly associated with this contrast of expectation and fact.

He writes: "That which is taken to be involved *in any event*, in every issue, *no matter what*, we are not aware of. If

we consider the entire field from bright focus through the
fore-conscious, the fringe, to what is dim, subconscious feeling, the focus corresponds to the point of imminent need, of
urgency; the fringe corresponds to things that have just been
reacted to or that will soon require to be looked after, while the
remote outlying field corresponds to what does not have to be
modified, and which may be dependably counted upon in dealing with imminent need. . . The *immediately* precarious, the
point of greatest immediate need, defines the apex of consciousness, its intense or focal mode."[7]

Dewey and Whitehead may not wholly agree in their
doctrines of consciousness. The interesting point is that according to both the distrust of knowledge is rooted in consciousness. Rather, consciousness is that distrustful feeling; the
feeling that theory may be in error; that purpose may not be
borne out by future events. To be self-conscious, i.e., to reflect upon your distrust of knowledge, is to feel the problem of
purpose.

Yet, one may fairly ask how in the light of our analysis of
process up to this point, such distrust could arise. Purpose
reflects the past and goes beyond the past to make a forecast
that the future will embody the peculiar qualitative unity of
the soul in this moment. And assuming continuity, as we have
been assuming it in this discussion of Whitehead, the future
does embody that forecast; the soul of this present moment
does remain on in future process. Purpose is always fulfilled;
the actual entity which it unified is given physical embodiment
in a future entity. On this analysis, theory could never be in
error; distrust of knowledge could never arise.

It is evident that the distrust of theory which informs consciousness springs from a further characteristic of process and
experience: discontinuity. Experience is precarious not because the soul continually advances into an ever wider and
more inclusive future, but because from time to time there is a
frustration of purpose and the future is narrower and poorer

than the past. So far as Whitehead recognizes this fact, he does it principally by introducing the notion of negative prehension.

*Negative Prehension*   Whitehead does not explain the notion of negative prehension clearly or in any detail; he does not seem to attach much importance to it. But it is possible to develop the notion by distinguishing three kinds of negation which he defines in various places.

One meaning of negative prehension is simply "exclusion from concrescence," or *mere diversity*. An actual entity is finite, including in the nexus from which it arises some actual entities and not including others. Hence, it includes some characteristics or forms of definiteness and does not include others. But this is merely one way of saying that it is different from other actual entities or possible ones. It is itself and not something else. The fact that it has a certain, determinate character implies that that character has limits. The fact that it is *this* also means that it is *not that*.

However, the fact that one actual entity is different from another does not mean that it is also incompatible with that other actual entity. That other actual entity is not included in its concrescence. Maybe it could have been included; maybe not. All that is being pointed out here is that the fact of diversity does not imply incompatibility. Indeed, the essence of creative advance is that "differents" are brought together in a concrescence which joins them in a single actual entity.

Whitehead appears to be using negative prehension in the sense of mere diversity when in *Adventures of Ideas* he speaks of it as "anaesthesia." However, in that work he also refers to negation as a positive fact, such as pain, horror, dislike. Here in what he calls *aesthetic destruction*, two incompatible feelings are present in a single subject without any reconciling factor. Here is active discord and conflict.

These two kinds of negation, mere diversity and aesthetic destruction, are not distinguished in *Process and Reality*. For there it is said that a negative prehension is a definite bond with the world and contributes its subjective form to the concrescence, though not the actual entity which it negatively prehends. However, it is hard to see how mere diversity, standing for the finiteness of the actual entity, can be thought of as a bond to that which is excluded. Certainly it cannot be conceived of as contributing a subjective form. For if bonds or relations mean anything according to Whitehead's theory, it is that the things bound together or related are really together. But the point about negative prehension is that two or more things really are *not* together. This is why there is an element of genuine pluralism in the world: some things are truly separate from one another.

However, if we think of negation in the sense of "aesthetic destruction" then we can see how such a prehension would contribute a subjective form to the concrescence. For the point about pain, for instance, is that then one feels some part of his flesh or spirit being torn away. He has that part, and yet something which is depriving him of it is also at work: he is losing a part of himself. Similarly pain may accompany the growing or creative process, as when, for instance, a man trying to state an idea which is practically within his grasp, for the moment feels it slipping away. Such conflicts and discords really can, for a while at least, exist within a person.

But they can exist only for a while. And this introduces a third sense of negation which must be stated, but which Whitehead says little or nothing about. The conflict of incompatibles cannot last: one or the other gains the upper hand —that is the significance of their being incompatible. When one of them does, then the other—so far as concerns the actual entity feeling the first thing—is lost and destroyed. Here is the kind of loss and destruction which has continually intruded itself on our discussion in this book. It is not the evil of finitude, nor the evil of pain and conflict, but the evil of *destruction and death*.

*Negation as Destruction*   Our analysis of process shows that much of the transiency of the world is illusory. Actual entities with their characteristics seem to pass out of existence, but in fact remain on in further stages of process. Putting it broadly, then, we can say that true stability in change is often the mode of alteration of things. But we must also include in our principles of process some account of the destruction of things and their characters.

How this comes about, it seems to me, can be stated in Whitehead's language. First, we must see that where destruction occurs in the course of a concrescence,[8] if a constituent feeling of a certain actual entity is eliminated, the unifying feeling of that entity must also be eliminated. For the unifying feeling prehends an eternal object which includes the eternal objects determining the subjective forms of the constituent feelings of the entity. Hence, if a constituent feeling is not admissible, neither can that unifying feeling be admissible which includes the excluded constituent feeling. Consequently we must think of destruction as involving elimination of the unifying feeling and some of its constituent feelings.

To illustrate: Two actual entities, *A* and *B*, have been associated with one another as actual entity, *A-B*, through several stages of process. In a further stage of process there is concrescence with actual entity *C*. In this further stage, *C* being compatible with *B*, concresces with *B* to form the actual entity *B-C*. But *C* is incompatible with *A* and so *A* and *A-B* are eliminated from the process which forms *B-C*. From the point of view of *B-C*, *B* is separated from its former association with *A*. This is the case of *evil as destruction*.

In a sense, this kind of elimination is merely another instance of mere diversity. *B-C*, as an atom of becoming, simply has nothing to do with *A* or *A-B*. But the important fact for us is that *B* has been associated with *A* in previous stages of process. Hence, insofar as *B-C* dissociates *B* from *A* this instance is distinguished from the case of mere diversity.

This account states the problem, and also suggests a solution. It suggests a way in which destruction may be overcome and made good. For while it shows that $A$ and the actual entity emergent from $A$-$B$ are lost in relation to $B$-$C$, the question of what happens to $A$-$B$ remains open. It may be that $A$-$B$, while it is lost in relation to $B$-$C$, still continues on in a process which connects it with other and compatible entities.

This suggestion involves the assumption that $B$ and its constituents can participate in the line of process of $A$-$B$ and also in the line of $B$-$C$; in short, that $B$, as an actual entity, can function in two different places. This, as we have seen, is a fundamental principle of Whitehead's account. A single actual entity can function in more than one continuum. Hence, it is possible that in one continuum an actual entity should be dissociated from an associate of long standing, while in another continuum the association of the two should continue.

In short, it is possible that the destruction and loss which our experience unquestionably records, is yet made good in a continuum beyond our experience. This Saving Order beyond experience, beyond history, beyond nature, which makes good the discontinuities of experience, history, and nature, Whitehead calls the Consequent Nature of God.

"The universe," writes Whitehead, "includes a threefold creative act composed of (i) the one infinite conceptual realization, (ii) the multiple solidarity of free physical realizations in the temporal world, (iii) the ultimate unity of the multiplicity of actual fact with the primordial conceptual fact."[9]

The first aspect is the Primordial Nature of God; the ordered realm of all possibility; in short, the Promise and the Word. The second aspect is the familiar pluralistic world of clashing men and events, coming into existence and going out of existence. The third aspect is the Consequent Nature of God, one actual entity whose conceptual pole is the Primordial Nature and whose physical pole is constituted by prehensions of the actual entities of the pluralistic world; in short, the Kingdom of Heaven. Let us consider the Primordial Nature and then the Consequent Nature of God.

*The Primordial Nature of God*  It is hard to try to write about the nature of God without deep embarrassment. Yet men have feelings and ideas of Him. Dim and shifting as these feelings and ideas may be, they are not without content. They are not of an unintelligible quiddity. They have a meaning which a man, while recognizing the pitiful inadequacy of his efforts, may yet try to clarify and communicate.

In our analysis of process we consider two aspects of the potentiality of an actual entity. First, we considered the unifying prehension which is the new factor in a concrescence. Secondly, we examined the conceptual prehensions which reproduce respectively the actual entities of the nexus. Strictly these two sorts of prehension exhaust the potentiality of the actual entity. But there is still a further kind of potentiality which is related to the actual entity. This is the potentiality of having consequences different from itself in the future, the fact that an actual entity may enter into further concrescences in many possible manners. Each actual entity has access to a realm of ordered potentiality which is not included in its conceptual pole. This realm is the power and purpose of the divine entity, the Primordial Nature of God.

Each concrescence is creative, bringing about the ingression of an eternal object hitherto unrealized in the nexus of this concrescence. This eternal object is derived not from the conceptual poles of any of the actual entities of its nexus, but from the Primordial Nature of God. But the Primordial Nature is also an actual entity and is physically prehended by every concrescence. So it is more accurate to say that the new conceptual prehension is derived from that physical prehension by which the subject prehends the Primordial Nature. It is correct to say that each concrescence is self-creative only if we include in its nexus the Primordial Nature.

The Primordial Nature of God does not destroy the private nature of the individual, atomic fact. The Primordial Nature, so to speak, is the great relater of things, providing that power which enables them to be really together in one another. This real togetherness does not destroy the individual "atom." The "atom" has its own peculiar character and in later stages of process continues to function in a relevant manner.

Whitehead's God, then, in one sense is *immanent*. The Primordial Nature enters into every concrescence. So far as an actual entity has the power to constitute a further actual entity, that power is God's power. Yet this power is also *imposed*. It is not the power of the atom of actuality itself, but only that power to which all actuality has access. There are these buds of experience and the Primordial Nature as the principle and power of budding does not obliterate its own creations.

Emerson stated the point in a simple image. "Spirit, that is, the Supreme Being," he wrote in *Nature*, "does not build up nature around us, but puts it forth through us, as the life of the tree puts forth new branches and leaves through the pores of the old. As a plant upon the earth, so a man rests upon the bosom of God."[10]

The Primordial Nature is the Promise. Our knowledge of it is the intuition that the world is governed by One Power. That knowledge must be an intuition, for it cannot be based on the evidence of history and nature. The processes of history and nature are not always continuous; they are infected with conflict and mortality. That is, each concrescence does not always reach a determinate outcome unifying all entities of the nexus. Sometimes there is conflict, loss, negative prehension. Yet our intuition of the Primordial Nature is the knowledge that as there is one creative power, so is there in the end one created order, the Consequent Nature of God.

*The Consequent Nature of God* Every actual entity, human and nonhuman, which has ever become is prehended by the Consequent Nature. Here there are no final incompatibilities. "In it there is no loss, no obstruction. . . The image—and it is only an image—the image under which this operative growth of God's nature is best conceived, is that of a tender care that nothing be lost."[11]

Here is that single, uninterrupted continuum which philosophers of progress seek for in vain in the events of our familiar, pluralistic world. In this single continuum, a single, complex purpose is realized in a single, complex act. There is neither past nor future, but only a present within which all events occur "all at once," *totum simul*, as subordinate parts of an all-inclusive whole.

In the temporal world there are negations in the mode of "mere diversity" and "destruction." But in the Consequent Nature, the excluded or destroyed entities are included. Here then is that Saving Order where all plans, all purposes, conscious or unconscious, are preserved and maintained. Here the creation, however slight, which the formation of each purpose involved is saved and used.

For the actual entity is not merely saved, but also used, by being joined with all other actual entities in a final synthesis. It is used as a constituent of the final integrations or "contrasts" which unify God's Consequent Nature. Its important contribution is not an eternal object, for all eternal objects are present eternally in the Primordial Nature. What an actual entity contributes to the Consequent Nature consists in the physical prehension of it by that Nature. These physical prehensions are necessary to God's nature. For they are the actualization of the parts of the Divine Purpose of which the Consequent Nature is the actualization of the whole. Because that purpose is power and plan there must occur its actualization in finite parts as the World. The whole cannot be actualized unless its parts are too. Hence, finite actualities are necessary to the infinite actuality.

The World needs God. It needs Him as the Single Purpose which provides its finite concrescences with creative power. But Whitehead's God is not a wholly transcendent deity which is external to, and independent of, the World and its parts. The World, the multiplicity of finite actualizations, is necessary to God, the unification of this multiplicity. Or to use other language: the multiverse is necessary to the universe. It is one mode of the fulfillment of the Purpose.

So when an actual entity is saved by and in this Consequent Nature, it is not only preserved but fulfilled. That Purpose which was immanent in it as the Primordial Nature is now actualized in the Consequent Nature. Hence the immortality of actual entities, conscious and unconscious, is personal only in a very restricted sense. In the Saving Order the finite entity is preserved, but also infinitely transformed. For "eternity will fulfill and not annul the richness and variety which the temporal process has elaborated."[12]

The relation of the Consequent Nature to human souls (as well as to other actual entities) is analogous to the relation of the soul to those various lines of process in the body from which it inherits. These lines of process, on the one hand, are inherited by the soul and, on the other, by the body in its interaction with the environment. But the analogy is very inexact. The bodily lines of process in their interaction with the environment may have futures which do not affect the soul. But all futures of a soul, whether inheriting from it in part or whole, are prehended by the Consequent Nature. Not only the soul's physical prehensions of its former moments, but also the soul's influence on body and environment are included within the Consequent Nature. That follows from the fact that the Consequent Nature is the coming together of every actual entity, simple or complex, soul or not soul. Hence, far more than bodily events within the soul, all events happen within God. They are all stages in the actualization of the Divine Purpose.

*Eros toward perfection* When we were previously examining the principles of concrescence, we started from a set of actual entities from which a new entity emerges. The course of the analysis brought out how these entities are integrated creatively in the emergent actuality. It may be that some of them cannot be integrated with the others, and so are negatively prehended. The "subjective aim" of the process, one might say, is to bring together as many actual entities as possible.

Whitehead does describe the subjective aim in such terms. He writes of it as "the urge towards the realization of the maximum number of eternal objects subject to the restraint that they must be under conditions of contrast."[13] By "contrast" he means relevance or compatibility. So what he is saying here is that the subjective aim is to realize as many eternal objects as the ordering of possibility—or "laws" of relevance —allows. Those actual entities whose unifying eternal objects are irrelevant to the other actual entities of the set from which the actuality is emerging, will be negatively prehended. So far as the unifying eternal objects of the entities are relevant or compatible; so far, that is, as there is an eternal object in the Primordial Nature which is their togetherness in the mode of potentiality, these subordinate eternal objects and their actual entities will be positivity included in the concrescence.

This aim at realizing more and more eternal objects, so long as there is a further eternal object which will unify them, Whitehead refers to as the aim at "balanced complexity." It can be thought of in less technical terms as an aim at "enrichment" or "intensity." It may also be called the "Eros toward perfection." The Eros is not a new force or further principle. It refers to a function of the Primordial Nature. The Primordial Nature is the final cause which pervades all process, realizing more and more of the possible and culminating in the perfect actuality of the Consequent Nature.

Whitehead's doctrine then is consistent with that of the aesthetic humanists who counsel men to enrich their souls; or, as Dewey puts it, to increase the shades and scope of meaning included in their present action. For where there is growth and enrichment, new finite actualities are being created. Hence,

any act of growth or enrichment is important because it is
doing a particular concrete task even though infinitesimal, in
the infinite concrete work which is set before us, the realization of the Primordial Nature.

*Evil as Negation*    That there is in some sense a Saving Order
is indicated by our moral and religious feelings. But is not the
notion of the Consequent Nature of God radically in conflict with the outlines of the Saving Order indicated by those
feelings, dim and abstract as those outlines are? In particular,
does not the Consequent Nature save "too much"? Putting
it bluntly, shall we say that the evil are saved as well as the
good?

We must turn to the root of the idea of evil: negative
prehension. In its most prominent sense, negative prehension is
destruction. It occurs when one actual entity of a concrescence is incompatible with another and results in the
elimination of certain of the constituents of one of the entities.
These eliminated actual entities are dissociated from the other
constituents and their unifying actual entity. We recognize
here the basic form of evil: something has been destroyed; a
man has been hurt or killed; one nation has been subjugated
by another.

But note wherein the evil lies. It lies not in the positive
character of any actual entity; each actual entity in itself,
that is, considered apart from its relations, is an actualization
of the possible and in some measure an enrichment of the
world. The evil lies in the destruction of such an actualization. It is a "negative fact." It actualizes nothing. Evil is
nothing; it is Non-Being.[14]

The murderer's act in itself may have a certain excellence
or art about it. The evil lies in its incompatibility with the
maintenance and growth of the higher powers of another man.
In itself the army of the aggressor has order and beauty, as
have all efficient things. War has a kind of aesthetic perfection,
if we can forget the suffering and frustration. "It is well this

is so terrible," said Lee as he watched the battle of Fredericks-
burg, "we should grow too fond of it."

Now, it would be ridiculous and immoral and treason
to the whole sense of this account of the world to jump to
the conclusion that the destructive men and forces of the
temporal world are not to be combated. Quite the contrary
follows, as our moral and religious feelings indicate. The
point which is being made here is the very simple one that the
"negative fact" of destruction cannot be saved in the Consequent Nature precisely because it is not a fact, not an actuality,
but the negation of fact and actuality. Negation exists only relative to parts of the temporal world. That is, negation is a
"fact" for those entities which have been dissociated from one
another. In the consequent Nature of God these dissociations
are superseded in the real togetherness of all actual entities of
all time and place.

But what of the evil purpose, the purpose which aims at
destruction? Is there not something in this purpose itself
which is evil? Yes, there is. Consider the aggressor. His purpose is in itself evil in the sense that it excludes elements of actuality which could have been included and so is poorer and
narrower than it might have been. That is, he is an aggressor
because he could have found a way to get along with his neighbor. It was humanly possible to find some compromise, some
reconciliation which would have adjusted his and his neighbor's interests. Inquiry, taking thought, reasoning together,
could have produced an adjustment in some measure adding
to the actuality of his purpose. But his purpose excluded these
real possibilities. Here there was negation in the mode of
diversity or exclusion.

If we reflect on this kind of negation for a moment, we see
that it characterizes all purpose, even that of the most humane
and tolerant man. No human purpose is or can be all-inclusive;
no human love universal. That is our finitude: we cannot know
enough to include in our purposes all purposes which are or
shall be. No matter how advanced the social system which we

support, it daily darkens hopes and frustrates growing powers which in some conceivable situation could be realized. There is a relative difference between the aggressor who could have found a reconciliation with his neighbor and the man whose best efforts and best knowledge cannot cope with some social problem. Yet this man of good will too carries a great burden of evil which in his pride he is inclined to forget. He too needs forgiveness.[15]

But who is this man of good will? He tries to find a reconciliation with his neighbor; he tries to promote the expression of creative powers wherever he can discern them. Such an effort is itself an additional trait of his purpose. Why should his purpose have this trait? How, in terms of Whitehead's analysis, could his purpose acquire this trait and this direction? This question is best approached through considering the grounds of faith. In the next chapter we shall consider the grounds of faith and what change faith may work in purpose.

## CHAPTER THIRTEEN

# FAITH AND MORALS

SUCH IS THE FLUENT WORLD OF MR. WHITEHEAD. THE TER-
minology is unfamiliar, but once that difficulty is overcome
it is easy to see that much of what he says is confirmed in
everyday experience. He sets out a system of very general
ideas which can be readily used to describe the movement of
human thought and action and natural process. Much is acceptable, but can we follow him to the very end? The crux
is: Are there grounds for believing there is one Divine Purpose
and Consequence? If there are not, the problem of purpose is
unsolved and we fall back into the arms of the skeptic and
defeatist.

"Proofs" of the existence of God are as presumptuous as
attempts to describe His nature. Yet that is because at bottom
we have an idea of His being and a faith in His existence which
mock the effort to catch them in our poor net of words. Once
we have caught a glimpse of this idea and this faith we see
why it is so hard to give them names. We cannot explain
why the effort is presumptuous until we have made the effort.

*Discontinuity as Dissociation*   The question is: Why accept
the hypothesis of the final real togetherness of all things
in which the discontinuity and destruction of the temporal
world are superseded? First, we must see that destruction
or discontinuity should be thought of as dissociation. Destruction occurs when some of the constituents of an actual entity
are eliminated. These constituents are dissociated from the
other actual entities with which they had previously been
unified. The hypothesis we are now considering is that this
dissociation is superseded in the Consequent Nature of God.

That hypothesis is implausible to common sense which rebels at the suggestion that a thing can be two "places" at the same "time." Whitehead's analysis of nature should have shaken the prejudice which prompts this reaction. In his fluent world an association of entities may continue to function in another continuum even though from the point of view of one of its constituents that association seems to have been broken up and destroyed.

This is a possibility which we must take seriously and it profoundly changes the nature of our problem. For now we must at least grant that there are two constructions which can be put on the fact of destruction. There is the possibility that the association has been utterly destroyed. There is also the possibility that it continues in another order of things. Hence our problem is not, What shall we say about the hard fact of utter destruction? but rather, Which construction shall we put upon the ambiguous fact of dissociation?

Perhaps this in itself is enough to solve the practical problem. The defeatist may rehearse the black record of death and failure which darkens the history of individual men and their societies. But if Whitehead's analysis of the common processes of nature is correct, the defeatist may never rest in his hopelessness and cynicism. The further suggestion must always be there that quite possibly the plain facts are not the true facts; that failure and death may be illusory.

*Self-transcendence* But we do not want to leave our inquiry in a state of hopeful indecision. We want to push it as far along the road toward conviction as we can. Do we find anything further in experience which gives a reasonable man grounds for honestly believing in a final unity?

Whitehead's theory of God indicates that there should be such grounds. Every actual entity includes a prehension of the Primordial Nature of God, the promise of a final unity. If this is so, then there should be some way in which a man can focus his attention upon that prehension and thereby discover in his experience a feeling and idea of final unity.

In a sense, we have been concerned with that prehension or feeling, throughout this book. We have constantly been concerned with that "element of futurity" or "principle of unrest" or "aspect of self-transcendence" which is a trait of all actuality. But this trait of actuality is precisely the conceptual pole of an actual entity which not only unifies the actual entity but also gives it access to the vast ordered realm of potentiality, the Primordial Nature.

Whitehead expresses this self-transcendence of things as a conclusion of modern physics.[1] Self-transcendence is a trait of history as well as of nature. The facts of history, like those of physical nature, refuse to be stable. Statesmen make a political settlement and guarantee it with all the harsh powers at their command. In a few years the facts of their settlement have given rise to strange and unexpected results, possibly the very opposite of what the planners had intended. No fact of existence is permanent. All facts are relative to something beyond themselves, as if they were in pursuit of some sufficiency or wholeness which they lack.

The soul itself displays a continual restlessness and an urge to become something more than it actually is. When we consider the notion of perspective, we note this. On the one hand, a man's perspective is his system of purpose as a complex unity. On the other hand, his perspective is riddled with ambiguity. It has many powers or potentialities which are not yet realized. Perspective is the point at which that which has been learned and accomplished touches a power drawing it on toward further accomplishment.

In the *Symposium* Plato makes it his principal theme to elucidate this restlessness and ceaseless movement of the soul. He calls this urge Love and the dialogue goes on the show how this passion, which seems to be deeply selfish, in fact aims at transforming those who share it. What the lover finds in union with the beloved is not his old nature over again, but rather something more than he had been, that state or end which drew him toward the beloved. For "everyone who desires, desires that which he has not already, and which is future and not present, and which he has not and is not, and of which he is in want."[2]

But the love of which Plato writes is not merely the attraction which draws one human being to another. It is that ceaseless urge which also drives them on toward self-completion in the ways of virtue, art, and contemplation; it is the Eros toward perfection. In the love of one human being for another, what we should see then is a parable for that Eros which in many and divers ways joins imperfect man and the perfect or complete being, God. "For," writes Plato, "God mingles not with man; but through Love all the intercourse and converse of God with man, whether awake or asleep, is carried on."[3]

A sense of this dissatisfaction which is yet the promise of a greater satisfaction has marked other philosophies in the Platonic tradition. "We grant that human life is mean," wrote Emerson in *The Over-Soul*, "but how did we find out that it was mean? What is the ground of this uneasiness of ours; of this old discontent? What is the universal sense of want and ignorance, but the fine innuendo by which the great soul makes its enormous claim? . . .

"The philosophy of six thousand years has not searched the chambers and magazines of the soul. In its experiments there has always remained, in the last analysis, a residuum it could not resolve. Man is a stream whose source is hidden. Always our being is descending into us from we know not whence. The most exact calculator has no prescience that somewhat incalculable may not baulk the very next moment. I am constrained every moment to acknowledge a higher origin for events than the will I call mine."[4]

It is the relativity and flux of things which is the great convincing fact. When we see that the facts are relative we see that they are not isolated and discontinuous, but that they are related to a further whole or unity. The "futurity" which is within them is precisely this unity at work in all its parts. It is the one final cause, the Primordial Nature of God, bringing the whole of process to fruition. Every moment of fact by its transiency proclaims itself to be only a part and therewith promises a unity beyond. The incompleteness, the poverty of the present facts, appears only because there is a completeness and wealth which they foretell.

We have a sense of the movement of things. This sense is not just the reflection of past experience that things do change. It is an immediate, present sense of the power which changes them. It is an immediate feeling, an intuition, of the completeness which all things aim at and will attain.

*The Idea and Feeling of Final Unity*    There is, it seems to me, an aspect of experience which indicates a final unity of things. Saints and philosophers have explored that aspect. Any proof or argument purporting to show that there is a final unity must connect itself with such experience, if it is to carry conviction.[5] That is, if the idea is to be convincing, it must be accompanied by or derived from a feeling of that unity. To be convinced of the existence of God is to feel His Presence. Proof will also be conversion. The best that words can do is to turn attention to this feeling. Yet, inadequate as our effort must be, we may nonetheless profitably examine the more intellectualist approach to the problem.

This approach is that we must believe that is a final unity, because we cannot deny that unity without asserting it. It is impossible, runs the argument, for a man to conceive of a final plurality of truth or fact, for if he will examine his conception of such a plurality, he will see that he holds this plurality to exist within a final unity. In short, there is in any thinking being a positive knowledge of the final unity of all things which his thought inevitably asserts, so to speak, regardless of his own wishes in the matter.

Suppose we make this statement: "The fundamental entities of the world are discontinuous with one another." The difficulty is that when we try seriously to accept this notion, we find ourselves putting these final pluralities into a still more final unity. We start out by thinking of the entities of the multiverse as simply separate and isolated from one another. But does this mean they are merely apart and with nothing whatsoever between them? This hardly seems acceptable. For if there is nothing between them, nothing whatever separating them, then are they not together? Or if there is something which separates them, which holds them apart, then will they not be really together by means of that which is really together with each?

As soon as we try to assert the existence of final pluralities they begin to develop relations with, or prehensions of, a common environment. Such pluralities will stay apart only when there is something to hold them apart relative to one another. And that which holds them apart relative to one another brings them together in a further unity. As F. H. Bradley writes: "We have no knowledge of a plural diversity, nor can we attach any sense to it, if we do not have it somehow as one."[6]

Or suppose we assert the familiar proposition: "All truths are relative." To say that a true proposition is relative means that this proposition holds of fact, but only in a certain context. When this context is eliminated, the proposition no longer holds. The connection asserted by the proposition holds so long as other connections are also present. The truth of this proposition depends upon other propositions also being true. With this view, incidentally, the general argument of this book would heartily agree. But the question here is what you mean when you say this is the case with all truths. What you mean is something like this: That if all truths could be examined each would be found to presuppose certain other truths. But obviously if all truths were somehow so examined, the resulting intelligence would include them in an organized system of truth which would not depend upon any true propositions outside itself since it would include all.

Here would be a final, unified, nonrelative system of truth. Did you not presuppose such a system when you asserted that all truths are relative? That is, did you not already presuppose that such a system exists in the mode of possibility, this is, could be known?

There is a natural objection: This is all the work of the mind. The mind cannot conceive of plurality without unity, nor of relativity without a whole to which all parts are relative. But that does not mean that the world is like that; just because the poor human mind finds a multiverse of truth or fact inconceivable tells us nothing about whether the world is or is not a multiverse. In this objection there is real point. It lights up the difficulty of arguing about such a subject. An argument can state what is inconceivable and what must be conceived. But it cannot carry conviction unless it directs the soul to the perception of a fact, the feeling of the final unity as God's presence in the soul. The best that argument can do is to show the stubbornness with which mind insists that this idea of final unity is really about fact.

For instance, let us follow this line of argument: A thing cannot be itself and also something else; If $A$, then $A$ and not $not\text{-}A$. When we examine any description of fact we insist that it conform to this principle if it is to be accepted as true, that is, as a description of fact. Theory may not be self-contradictory, because fact cannot be self-contradictory. Truth is self-consistent because it is the truth about a self-consistent reality. The mind stubbornly insists on the principle of identity and noncontradiction as a character of true theory and real fact. Yet, as we have noted throughout this book and especially in the discussion of Whitehead, no theory and no fact with which we are acquainted is self-consistent. Every theory we develop in inquiry presupposes further propositions which it is the effort of further inquiry to elicit. Every actual entity is itself and also its consequences. It is not just itself, but inseparably more and other than itself. Like our theories about actuality, an actual entity is self-contradictory. We conclude that these apparent facts are not fact, an absurdity. Or we conclude that there is an Ultimate Fact including all apparent facts which is self-consistent. The principle of identity and noncontradiction, bare formal notion that it is, is one form taken by our positive knowledge of that final unity of all things.

It seems that we cannot help but criticize and depreciate our knowledge of the world. Our science is an abstraction; it is incomplete and inadequate. Yet we can so criticize and depreciate only because we feel there is a knowledge which is complete and adequate. Every separate truth is incomplete because we know there is a complete truth in the light of which, in whose illumination, it would be shown to be incomplete. In our incomplete knowledge there is also present an idea and feeling of that knowledge which is complete. It is this idea which is the source of our ceaseless, Faustian discontent with what we now know and purpose.

We complain that the world is uncertain. Whence comes this notion of certainty by which we measure the things of this world and find them wanting? If we have experience only of the uncertain, how do we acquire a notion of the certain? We observe that human judgment is fallible, that truth is relative, that man is mortal. Do these terms, fallible, relative, mortal, have meaning? If they do, must we not grant that their meanings involve notions of the infallible, the absolute and the immortal? For the former terms are merely the negation of the latter. And if we do have notions of the infallible, the absolute, and the immortal, how can we explain the origin of such notions? Do we not derive them from experience? Are they not the fine innuendo by which the great soul makes its claim? That is a question which a man must answer for himself.[7]

*Self-consciousness* A conscious feeling is an integration of a propositional feeling and a physical feeling. Its subjective form is the contrast between theory, what might be, and fact, what is. Already in this contrast there is a distrust of knowledge. To reflect upon this distrust is a further stage of feeling, self-consciousness. In this further stage the conscious feeling is integrated with the feeling of God. The subjective form of the self-conscious feeling is at once a greater doubt and a resolution of that doubt in certain hope. There is a greater fear and doubt when the distrust of theory is contrasted with the feeling of the immense unrealized powers of the world, the Primordial Nature of God. There is certain hope in the contrast of these feelings with the feeling of God's Consequent Nature. Skepticism, radical doubt, fear, are the beginning of wisdom. For that great fear can come only from a source in which all may trust.

As a conscious being, man is creative. In this role he is an intelligent animal, the tool-user and scientist, *homo faber* and *homo sapiens*. His power to retain, organize, and reflect upon past experience gives him creativity of an exceptionally high order. In this role, he is concerned with "natural fact" only, whether he is dealing with physics, chemistry, medicine, economics, sociology, or political science. The question he asks is, How can I more efficiently achieve my present ends-in-view? In the course of successful inquiry, he at once conforms to and conquers nature. He does not simply adjust himself to his environment; he also adjusts the environment to himself. He reconciles his ends with fact and fact with his ends. There-fore, he at once acquires greater freedom by his conquest of nature and develops his own nature by enrichment of his ends.

As an intelligent animal he may also be a social animal. He may find that his ends are promoted by forming common purposes with others; that coöperation gets results. He may, therefore, seek reconciliation with others and thereby realize more of his powers. So in his role of intelligent animal, man also is a culture-building animal. Throughout, it must be emphasized, his ends-in-view are developed and his self is being realized. The Eros drives him continually toward greater excellence.

But man is not only a critic of means to ends. He is also a critic of ends. He seeks not only more efficient means, but also the right ends. He asks not only, "What is useful for me?" but also, "What am I useful for?" He is not only an intelligent animal, but also a moral animal; not only a scientist, but also a philosopher. He is not only conscious, but also self-conscious.

In self-conscious reflection a man arrives at an intuition that the world is creative and one. This intuition is not only an idea, but also a feeling. It is a feeling that he is a creative agent of that greater creative process; that its purpose is also his purpose; that God's will is also his own deeper will. This intuition not only leads man to see the creative unity of things; it also leads him to try to promote it. To know that God is, is at the same moment to will His will. To be self-conscious is to be a critic of ends. The religious intuition is also a source of an ethical imperative. What is the content of this imperative?

*Solution of the Problem of Purpose*  To begin with, the imperative of this ethics is that the creativity of the soul is good and is to be promoted. The human soul is one of the manifestations of that great creative power which pervades the universe. The soul does not merely register conformally what is presented to it, but rather works up that material into its plans and purposes. Intelligence is creative, and these plans of ours, derived from the given facts, but always going beyond those facts, are its creations. In them there ingress into actuality eternal objects which previously had lain unrealized in the Divine Purpose. In the course of successful inquiry, the soul is enriched in shades and scope of meaning of present action.

The vocation of man is the pursuit of knowledge. He ought

to act on his most probable knowledge because action is the only way in which the continuous growth of knowledge can occur. Indeed, he cannot be said to know unless he tries to act. For the effort to act, i.e., purpose, is the unifying factor of the soul at any moment. A soul without purpose literally disintegrates into its less complex constituents. Defeatism, a refusal to act on one's most probable knowledge and a falling back on the more conventional and less complex expectations, is this disintegration of the soul.

Here is the solution of the problem of purpose: A man ought to act on his most probable knowledge because in forming a purpose on such knowledge an element of possibility is actualized in his soul and because only by acting can the further growth of knowledge occur.

History may frustrate our purposes. We can never have certainty about what will happen in the temporal world. The temporal world is a destructive as well as a creative world. Yet that fact cannot shake our faith that in the end somehow all souls are saved and used. Indeed, a certain contempt for what happens in the temporal world and in history must accompany this faith. The things of this world are fortuitous and swiftly perishable. The gratification of human wishes, your own or others', can never be your final standard, although you must work unceasingly to achieve that gratification.

For the whole sense of this faith is lost if you allow your detachment to degenerate into passive resignation. Merely to accept the world; to fail to learn from it; to give up trying to change it—this perverts hideously the very premise from which your feeling of detachment follows. That premise is that this world is a place for the making of souls. As such, it is an immensely important place.

Our faith is that our efforts to change the world will surely bear fruit. Because of that faith nothing can make our hopes flag. No frustration, no disaster, no dark inference of inevitable decline can diminish our strenuous reformism. We are at peace only because we know that our work surely counts. We are intensely attached to this world precisely because of our faith in the next. Such a faith will not tolerate defeatism in the guise of religious resignation.

This otherworldly faith gives eternal importance to the things of this world, to fallible human knowledge and transient human purpose. Its ethics is not an empirical ethics, but it is the ethics of empiricism. Knowledge gained from experience— empirical science in the broad sense—is an unreliable instrument for controlling nature and making history. But as the content of human purpose, this science contributes lastingly to the Saving Order. Our continual efforts to unlock the secrets of nature and to extend the bounds of science are of the essence of that process of making souls which is the great work of the world. And if our age is a more scientific age than any other, then in a real sense it is a more devout age.

*The Ethics of Humanity*  Our faith gives us a reason for acting on our best knowledge. It solves the problem of purpose, the problem of the relativity of truth. That problem, as stated in Chapter II, was not an ethical problem. Yet we have seen that the solution to it involves an ethics. A man cannot gain that faith which makes sense of his knowledge and purpose without at the same time feeling an ethical imperative. The solution to the problem of purpose is an ethical and ultimately a religious solution. My creative inquiry is worth while because creativity everywhere is worth while. My pursuit of truth is important because the pursuit of truth by men anywhere is important. Therefore, it is my duty not only to seek truth and excellence on my own part, but also to help others seek truth and excellence. If my soul's growth is important, so is their souls' growth.

This ethics is not unlike the ethics of civilization, yet there is an important difference of emphasis. The ethics of civilization began with the obligation of man to seek community with other men. In the course of the argument, we were obliged to grant that this obligation alone did not satisfy our moral feelings and that there is also an obligation for a man to develop his skills and powers. The argument went on to show that these two obligations are often compatible, since the obligation of community can be expressed in reconciliation which itself develops the purposes reconciled.

There is an important aspect of moral feeling which the ethics of civilization fails to include. We do feel obliged to seek reconciliation; we know that when we develop new ties of coöperation with others our own knowledge is increased and our own powers and skills heightened. But we also feel an obligation to help others even where no common purpose can be developed.

A man may be a stranger to us; perhaps we shall never see him. Yet if he is in need, we have an obligation to help him. He is not a fellow member of a community. His purposes do not supplement ours in a common pattern of action. His purposes may be informed by the outlandish customs of another part of the globe, or another section of the city. In spite of sharing certain general elements of a common humanity, he may look at things with a perspective which makes his thoughts incommunicable to us. Yet we feel we have an obligation to him. For he too has a duty of self-realization and, different as his personal adventure may be from ours, we ought to help him if he is in need. We feel an obligation to man as such.[8]

The faith to which the philosophy of creative advance leads enables us better to understand this aspect of moral feeling. This faith implies a duty to promote the growth of creative powers in any and all men. It implies a duty to develop your own powers, and a duty to seek reconciliation, and a duty to man as a creative being. We may call this ethics the ethics of humanity.

The ethics of humanity is not incompatible with the ethics of civilization. It sets the ethics of civilization in a different light. The ethics of humanity, so to speak, begins with the individual. It recognizes how deeply the individual can be developed by community. But it does not make community an end in itself. Community is a means to the rational self-realization of the individual. But that self-realization may be promoted by acts of helpfulness and generosity which need not create ties of community. This ethics is a Kantian, an Hegelian, but, even more, a Christian ethics.

Common purpose is one means to the self-realization of the individual. But it must be emphasized that no group or society of this temporal world can be a community in the full Rousseauist sense. It cannot be a community in which each of the members surrenders his whole personality to the common purpose and receives it back as an indivisible part of the whole. In this pluralistic world, there will always remain a part or aspect of the personality which is separate and isolated and incommunicable to the group.

Examine the most intimate relationships which exist between people and you will see this fact. Husband and wife; parent and child; friend and friend; family, home-town, and neighborhood, not to mention church, trade-union, or country: in none of these relationships is there a complete surrender of the personality of all to all; in none is there complete understanding. After all the social ties have been reckoned up and all the identities of purpose noted, there remains a solitariness in each man which leaves him something of a mystery to anyone else.

There is a perfect community of real togetherness in which we are all members one of another. But that society cannot be on earth; it is heaven. One of the impracticalities of secular thought such as Rousseau's is to imagine that earth can be heaven. Only to this final community and to the Purpose which is making it from the materials we help provide do we owe unconditional loyalty, not to any earthly community now or later. To say this is merely to express the obvious sense of the moral feelings that above the law of the state and the customs of society there is a Higher Law.

*The Law of Reason*   This Higher Law is the Law of Reason. Our sense of this Higher Law springs from an intuition of the ultimate rationality of the world. This intuition takes various forms in the mind and so gives rise to various meanings of the term reason. In its most modest form it consists of the elementary principles of traditional logic. Men usually retain a belief in these principles of reason even when they have surrendered the hope of finding a standard of ethics or an idea of the final nature of reality. A feeling that theory ought to conform to the demands of logical truth, a feeling of "logical necessity," remains, although such a feeling must be something of a mystery so long as you refuse to examine the ethical and metaphysical ideas which logic points toward.

For, the principles of reason expressed in logic point beyond themselves. The mind insists that these principles are about fact; that ultimately fact must conform to them. And this insistence of the mind, as we have seen, leads toward the insight that the world is ultimately a self-consistent whole.[9] Likewise, the moral feelings indicate that human conduct is subject to an imperative whose content is similar to the principles of reason expressed in logic. The imperative of reason can be interpreted in various ways: the principles of intelligent inquiry and rational self-realization; the ethics of community; the ethics of civilization; the ethics of humanity. Each attempts to express the larger idea of reason underlying our moral feelings. In the philosophy of creative advance we approach an adequate expression of this larger idea of reason, this insight that the world is a creative universe in which man has his special duty to perform.

The ethics of humanity is the ethics of the man of good will. The effort to follow the imperative of this ethics is that trait of purpose which makes him a man of good will. Yet the man of good will bears a great burden of evil and the sharper his sense of his duty the more heavily will that burden rest on him. The imperative he tries to obey is vastly beyond his power ever to satisfy. He is continually faced with conflicting duties. To satisfy one is to neglect the other. He has duties to himself, his family, his neighbors, and to the stranger who is everywhere. Each duty demands unlimited attention. If his efforts are to be in any measure effective he must associate himself with some social system and with some government. Yet the visible imperfections and cruelties of any society and government in history are profound. And beyond the evils he can see are those he cannot see but must suspect, the evil consequences of well-meant plans, the untoward results to which the satisfactory institutions of one age lead in the next. In the light of these inevitable facts, he would be a cynic if it were not that the very feeling which enables him to discern these evils at the same time assures him that his effort is worth while. His good will, sincere as it may be, cannot give him peace. He too needs forgiveness.

# CONCLUSION

# CHAPTER FOURTEEN

# POLITICS

THE PHILOSOPHY OF CREATIVE ADVANCE SOLVES THE PROBLEM of purpose. It arms a man against irrationalism and defeatism. In the same moment it defines his duty and orders him into action. The philosophy of creative advance entails the ethics of humanity. To accept the consolations of that philosophy is also to assume the heavy burdens of this ethics.

The argument has been abstract and often, no doubt, wrong-headed. Yet I doubt that the reader will find it irrelevant to the immediate problems of government and society today. A virtue of our age is that it drives the mind to follow through the urgent problems of the moment toward deeper truths, in which a more secure and confident age might not take an interest. How far the insights of the philosophy of creative advance approach any deeper truth the reader will judge. It is also for him to determine how to use these insights when deliberating the problems of the day.

The main outlines of the political theory implied by this philososphy should already be fairly clear. Obviously, that political theory is utterly at variance with the principles of fascism, nazism, and other political forms of irrationalism. It is also hostile to Marxian communism. On the other hand, the socialist or liberal or conservative should find neither the politics nor the ethics nor the metaphysics of this book incompatible with his own political and social program. The general principles which have emerged from our argument can be shared by men of very divergent political beliefs.

Such a book as this cannot, and should not, end with a party manifesto. Yet it should be of use to men trying to formulate their own political theory and take a stand on issues which demand partisanship. How the central ideas of this book might be used, what their main lines of relevance to politics seem to be, where the resulting political theory is like and unlike certain traditional theories, it will be the task of these concluding pages briefly to indicate.

*Collectivist Ethics*   The philosophy of creative advance obviously owes a great deal to metaphysical idealism. But the ethics of humanity stands in sharp contrast with a type of ethics which may justifiably be called traditional idealist ethics. One is individualist; the other collectivist. As a result, there is a critical difference in political theory.

Let me summarize the position which I attribute to certain idealists and with which I wish to differ: Self-realization occurs only when a man forms common purposes with other men. The good life for the individual lies wholly in a common life shared with others and governed by a common purpose. Purposive activity which does not express, or is not directed toward forming, a common purpose is not an element of the good life or of self-realization. No aspect of self-realization is private, nonsocial, individual. It follows for political theory that the essential purpose of the state is to promote community among the members of the state. It may also be held to follow that the state is truly a state only so far as its members are bound together in a common purpose.

Such a collectivist ethics, its seems to me, is expressed or implied in the works of most British idealists. Bosanquet's *Philosophical Theory of the State* is a particularly striking example. What Bosanquet means by "the best life" for the individual he does not make entirely clear.[1] But it is abundantly evident that, whatever it is, the best life can flourish only as an integral or organic part of a common life. In the true state, the mind of the individual is wholly social. Bosanquet writes: "Each individual mind, if we consider it as a whole, is an expression or reflection of society as a whole from a point of view which is distinctive and unique." Conversely, the state or social whole is "a whole consisting of psychical dispositions and their activities, answering to one another in determinate ways. It would therefore be of the nature of a continuous or self-identical being, pervading a system of differences and realised only in them. It differs from a machine, or from what is called an 'organism' pure and simple, by the presence of the whole in every part, not merely for the inference of the observer, but, in some degree, for the part itself, through the action of consciousness."[2]

Here Bosanquet is restating Rousseau's formula of community: each member of the state community has surrendered his entire personality to the community and received it back as an organic part of the whole. Any actual state, so far as it is a state, is such a community. The system is never quite harmonious; readjustment is continually going on. But the essential purpose of any actual state is to approximate this ideal; that is, to make the community more of a community.

The philosophy of creative advance, as I have tried to interpret it, rejects this organic theory of the state and the collectivist ethics on which it is founded. One reason is that society is not, and cannot be, an actual entity. Society is not, and cannot be, a *moi commun*, a common self. In any individual soul there is in some resepcts and some measure a real togetherness with other souls. But there is no over-soul which includes these related souls, except God. There is a perfect community in which we are all members of one another. But that community cannot be on earth; it is heaven.

We have previously argued this point on the grounds of common experience. Even the most intimate relationships, one must admit, fall far short of complete community, that is, complete mutual understanding and unconditional loyalty. But there is a further reason why complete community cannot be achieved among men. The very fact that each soul is a center of creative process prevents it. All souls in great measure merely reflect social influences; perhaps some are wholly lacking in individuality and do no more than reproduce conformally these influences. But where reason has started to work, where there is intelligent inquiry and reflection, the soul begins to display traits and purposes which are its own unique creations. They may be modest, hardly passing beyond the stage of inarticulate daydreams. They may be the sudden insights of genius, or the slow fruition of laborious investigation. But they are the soul's own.

This creative process is at once the most precious part of a man and something that sets him apart from others. It expands his mind, alters the contours of his purposes, and so undermines the common ground which previously enabled him to communicate. In time, mutual understanding may be reestablished, but creativity continually threatens to disrupt it. Even if a man could be united in a perfect community of purpose with others, the creative advance of his soul would throw his purposes out of harmony with the common purpose; his new perspective would make him something of a stranger to his former friends. Indeed, one thing that makes close friendship attractive is that it is never perfect. Friend never completely understands friend, but each is attracted to the other by the changing insights into truth which the symbols of communication occasionally reflect from one mind to the other. So far as men are rational, that is, creatively intelligent, they can never participate wholly in one another's lives.

Moral collectivism makes its ideal a society in which each person is entirely absorbed into the life of the whole. Ethically this idea is wrong. If, *per impossibile*, it were achieved, it would involve destroying the essential humanity of man, his reason. In fact, such a society cannot be achieved and the effort to create it can, at most, establish only a social unity which is false and therefore oppressive.

The philosophy of creative advance rejects moral collectivism. It rejects the theory that self-realization occurs only in and through the formation of common purposes. The ethics of humanity starts from the individual. His personal adventure in the pursuit of truth has value and importance, regardless of whether his insights are derived from, or communicated to, society. If he were the only man on earth he would have his duty, and his performance of duty would have eternal meaning. The metaphysics of this philosophy is collectivist, but its ethics and politics are strenuously individualist.

*Individualist Ethics*   The ethics of humanity has more in common with the thought of many empiricist philosophers than it has with the thought of many idealists. For John Stuart Mill, for example, the vocation of man is the exercise of creative intelligence. "It is," he writes in his essay on Liberty, "the privilege and proper condition of a human being, arrived at the maturity of his faculties, to use and interpret experience in his own way. . . . He who lets the world, or his own portion of it, choose his plan of life for him, has no need of any other faculty than the ape-like one of imitation. He who chooses his plan for himself, employs all his faculties. He must use observation to see, reasoning and judgment to forsee, activity to gather materials for decision, discrimination to decide, and when he has decided, firmness and self-control to hold to his deliberate decision."[3]

In this essay Mill is concerned with intelligent inquiry as the manner in which the human personality grows. Like Dewey he also applied this general notion to the narrower field of professional scientific inquiry. In that part of his *Logic* in which he discusses induction he sets out the principles by which truth is discovered, verified, and developed. His "canons of induction" and his discussion of them are technical. Yet the central idea is the same as that underlying the essay on Liberty.

On this notion of creative intelligent inquiry, Mill founded the political theory of his essay on Liberty. In this notion he found a standard which determined the proper functions of government. The functions which Mill allowed government in this essay are far too limited to satisfy us today. But the principle from which he started does not necessarily lead to *laisser-faire*, is still useful and convincing, and in general agrees with the doctrine of rational self-realization stated in this book. It agrees in general with this doctrine, yet it springs from a radically different philosophy. This difference is worth considering in order to illustrate the use, indeed, the necessity of metaphysics to political theory.

*Metaphysics and Ethics*   In Mill's essay on Utilitarianism, his thought departed radically from Bentham's pleasure-philosophy. "Quantity of pleasure being equal," Bentham had written, "pushpin is as good as poetry." But Mill admitted, or rather insisted, that pleasures differ not only in degree, but also in kind. This destroys the central idea of the pleasure-philosophy. There is no longer a single motive or drive behind all human action, the desire for pleasure. Not the quantity of pleasure determines what a man will do, but the structure of fundamental appetites.

One vital link remained. Mill like Bentham vigorously opposed any suggestion that man has a "moral faculty"[4] or that moral obligation is "a transcendental fact."[5] He claimed to base his ethics of politics, not on a moral law which is in any sense intuitive or *a priori*, but rather on the observed facts of the fundamental tendencies or appetites of human nature. He held that it is the "privilege and proper condition" of man to pursue truth through intelligent inquiry, not because such action is dictated by metaphysical or religious insight, but because such action fulfills an "inward tendency" of human nature. "Human nature," he wrote, "is . . . a tree, which requires to grow and develop itself on all sides, according to the tendency of the inward forces which make it a living thing."[6]

The "tendency of the inward forces" of human nature: How does one go about discovering what this is? On what ground would Mill choose to defend his conclusions about the inner nature of man? He excludes the ground of rational intuition or religious insight. The implication appears to be that his conclusions are derived from, and could be verified by, observation and experiment. Mill's procedure, in short, is to base his ethics on what we might call a "science" of human nature.

So long as scientific investigations of human nature arrive at conclusions like Mill's, no liberal democrat or decent man will seriously object to the ethics derived from these conclusions. But suppose a careful inquiry into the nature of the psyche shows that its tendencies are quite different from what Mill believed. Suppose, for instance, this inquiry shows that man has an innate instinct of aggression, deeper and more powerful than his instinct to pursue truth. If the political theorist is still to follow Mill's procedure, he must alter his ethics of politics to allow expression to this newly discovered tendency. He should conclude that government ought to do more to provide opportunities for men to abuse and injure one another. For a model of the ideal society, he may look back to the days of tournaments, trial by battle, and private war.

To let Mill's ethical procedure carry one to such conclusions is silly and fascistic. But it is not silly to suppose that scientific inquiry into the psyche may bring to light inward tendencies antagonistic to intelligent inquiry. Such a discovery would shatter an ethics like Mill's because that ethics rejects metaphysics and religion. It could not touch the essentials of the ethics of humanity precisely because this ethics has a metaphysical and religious foundation.

If men have an instinct of aggression, it is better to know about that instinct that not to know about it. In that sense, the ethics of humanity would welcome the discovery of such an instinct. For, so far as such a discovery revealed the mode of behavior of this instinct, we should get some hint of how to control it or mitigate its effects. This ethics is not to be daunted by the revelation of forces of destruction in nature or human nature. It is founded on a philosophy which at once acknowledges that discontinuity is a basic trait of the temporal world and insists that the duty of man is to struggle against discontinuity. Fidelity to the principles of intelligent inquiry, regardless of what such inquiry may find in the psyche, is a dictate of the moral imperative.

So far then the political theory of the ethics of humanity is like and unlike the traditional views of idealists and empiricists. The essential individualism of the theory should be clear. But a word of caution is necessary. The word individualism has many meanings. As it is used here it does not mean that the self or soul is, or should be, wholly self-contained, "enclosed as it were in an impervious globe." The individual cannot, and should not, be absorbed wholly in the common life. But he will find community a source of enrichment and stands under an obligation to communicate to others, so far as possible, the results of his mental and spiritual growth. Bosanquet's theory of the state as a complete community is an exaggeration. But it is an exaggeration which points to an important fact. It is a fact that some aspects of a man's personality are involved in common purposes with others. It is a fact that such common purposes are one means of self-realization.

We have examined these facts in our discussion of the ethics of community and civilization. We have seen that where men are united by common purpose, each understands his role and the roles of others and how these complementary functions are joined in a unified pattern of social conduct. We have seen that reconciliation by forming new ties of community enlarges mutual understanding and the powers and skills of the participants. Obviously, such relationships are wide and deep in any society. How widely they extend through a society, and how deeply they involve its members, are questions for careful empirical inquiry. Here we wish merely to show the relevance of such relationships to political theory.

Common purpose is a means of self-realization. As the idealists assert, government therefore ought to take care to protect and promote common purpose. The voluntary associations of modern society often heighten and enrich the inner life of their members. So far as they do, government should favor them. Government ought to do this, not because participation in a common life is the only means of living the good life, but because it is one means of achieving the good life.

*Natural Law*   The state is not, and should not be, an all-absorbing, a perfect community. But should it be a community in a looser sense? Should it be a community in the sense that all its members are agreed on certain general objectives of government? Consider the general objectives stated by the ethics of humanity. May we not say that the members of the state, so far as they try to fulfill this imperative, are united by a common purpose?

The term may be, and often is, used in this sense. But such usage, it seems to me, stretches the term unduly and obscures the most useful meaning which can be attached to it. "Common purpose," and "community," as I prefer to use them, refer to the integration of certain aspects of human personalities. This use is obscured if these terms are also used to refer to the general identity of purpose which arises when men accept the moral imperative. Men have duties to one another, even if they are not, even if they cannot be, in community with one another. The stranger and the alien may demand our help even though they stand outside the "general will." Simply as rational beings, men have rights and duties toward one another. Normally, men will look for the definition of their rights and duties to the customs and purposes of their society. But the "general will" is not soverign; it cannot claim unconditional loyalty. Man has access to a higher seat of social criticism and self-criticism, namely, reason. And the school of political theory which best understands and expresses this fact, it seems to me, is neither the idealist nor the empiricist school, but the natural rights school.

The moral imperative states a Higher Law, the Law of Reason. This Law imposes upon man the duty of self-realization; it thereby gives him a right to self-realization and a duty of respecting and protecting that right in others. As the natural rights school has always argued, these rights and duties are" antecedent" to government. Some particular society may not recognize them. The people controlling the government of that society may not recognize these rights and duties; the people subject to the government may not claim them. Indeed, no government can fully realize the objectives imposed on it by these rights and duties. Like any particular man, any government must fall short of the demands of the Law of Reason. Yet these rights and duties remain the eternal rights and duties of man.

But is it proper to call this Law of Reason natural law and these rights and duties natural? Does this not confuse the moral law which God imposes on man with the "laws" of nature which man discovers in empirical inquiry? So far as the use of the term "natural" results in this confusion, the objection is sound. But there is an important sense in which the Law of Reason is natural. It is not natural if by that you mean that scientific inquiry will inevitably show that the inner tendency or basic drive of human nature is to follow reason. But scientific inquiry shades off into philosophical inquiry. The inquiry of conscious man when turned to the study of his own nature in its immediacy tends to become the inquiry of self-conscious man, bringing to light the presence of God in man. And the God which self-conscious inquiry finds is a God who is not only imposed on the world, but also immanent in the world.[7] The Law of Reason is not only a moral law given to man, but also a law which is natural to man because it springs from his own deepest nature.

The Law of Reason gives man the right and duty of rational self-realization. The idea expressed in this Law can be grasped with some clarity, but it is highly abstract. From it alone nothing can be deduced about the form which any particular human institution or government should take. It presents us with a general end-in-view which we must then apply to the existing facts and the possibilities we have discovered in these facts.

The Law of Reason cannot tell us what part of the people should have the vote; whether property should be owned by individuals or by government; what civil liberties should be guaranteed; whether the government of any particular society should be democratic, aristocratic, or dictatorial. Our duty is to support that institution which seems least imperfect under the circumstances. It would have been wrong to introduce universal suffrage into twelfth-century England; it would be wrong to narrow the suffrage in modern Britain. It would have been wrong to nationalize industry in Jefferson's America; it might be wrong not to nationalize it in the event of another great depression in the United States. Under some circumstances, dictatorship may be the only way in which the foundations of civilized society can be preserved or constructed. There are no eternal forms of government or human law.

Even in the more civilized states the Law of Reason will be embodied in a set of political and social institutions which is only a distant approximation, a partial interpretation, of the ideal. Frustrations and cruelties, known and unknown, present and imminent, will disfigure all states. But while a state cannot be made perfect, it can be made better. Our duty is continually to work for a less partial embodiment of the Law of Reason.

*Democracy* We are to work for improvement. But who is to say what is better and what is worse? In interpreting the Law of Reason, who is to judge?

Western civilization has developed a form of government which, where it has been practicable, has given an answer morally more satisfactory than those given by other known forms. This form of government is democracy, i.e., government in which control and direction are substantially in the hands of the adult population. In a democratic government the task of interpreting the Law of Reason lies with the people, organized for discussion and decision.

The first virtue of a democratic government is that it has

an unrivaled knowledge of the important facts. These are not merely the facts about what people are doing and how they do it—the external facts, so to speak, such as statistics on income and trade or the behavioral descriptions of economics and other social sciences. The important facts also include how people feel; what these external facts mean as elements in the pains and pleasures, frustrations and successes of human purpose—the internal facts.[8] So far as a government is democratic, it bases its decisions upon these important facts.

Yet each man's view of the facts is distorted by perspective, by individual and group bias. In a democracy, therefore, the people are organized for discussion and decision in institutions of various kinds, formal and informal, private and public. Out of the competition of partial truths, the process of discussion, it is hoped, will produce a wider and more inclusive truth.[9] When such discussion is successful, as A. D. Lindsay remarks, "the narrowness and one-sidedness of each person's point of view are corrected and something emerges which each can recognize as embodying the truth of what he stood for, and yet (or rather therefore) is seen to serve the purpose of the society better than what anyone conceived for himself."[10]

And this is the second virtue of democracy: that it tries to utilize the creative intelligence of all its citizens. So far as a government is democratic, it mobilizes, for the struggle with common problems, a greater fraction of the brain-power of the society. Perhaps the matter can be put this way: If a society did produce or constitute a common mind, a *moi commun*, there would be no problem of government. For then the society, like the mind of an individual, could observe, reflect, decide without the mediation of institutions (although even the individual mind cannot do without its habits of rational thought). But since there is not, and cannot be, a common social mind, the problem is, so to speak, to create a machine which will do the same work. The problem is so to organize the individual minds of the society that each shall contribute all its power to the process of thinking and deciding and the effect, if not the reality, of a common mind shall be achieved.

This view of democracy and of the relation of democracy to the Natural Law is not far from the theory of John Locke. According to Locke, there is "a law of Nature . . . which obliges everyone, and reason, which is that law, teaches all mankind who will but consult it" what the rights and duties of man are. If men did not recognize the Law of Reason, government would be the product of force and violence, and men would live together "by no other rules but that of beasts, where the strongest carries it."[11] But since men do, as a general rule, recognize that Law, there is "another rise of government, another original of political power."[12] For even with men of good will, anarchism is impracticable. Even men who recognize the Law of Reason will yet disagree on its interpretation, being "partial to themselves and their friends," when they are judges in their own cases. Therefore, they seek an "impartial judge" who will administer the Law without bias.

Where shall men find an "impartial judge?" Locke did not think one would be found in any single man or select group of men. He was thoroughly disabused of any belief in "dominion by grace," ecclesiastical or political.[13] The only judge whom he would trust was "the people." Not that the only true government is direct democracy in which the people make all the decisions as a body. The people may adopt any form of political organization which they find expedient. But final direction and control rest in them. "Who shall be judge," wrote Locke, "whether prince or legislative act contrary to their trust? . . . To this I reply, the people shall be judge."[14] To the people, exercising the rights of free speech and discussion, final judgment is reserved.

Discussion, the essence of democracy, may not be successful. It may not lead to a reconciliation of opposing views, but may exacerbate differences and make a *modus vivendi* more difficult, as the public wrangling between Northern and Southern extremists before the Civil War may have done.

The characteristics of a society may be such that the attempt to follow democratic procedures would have disastrous results. For instance, consider the possibilities if complete democracy were introduced into Germany, Japan, or Russia today. Experience has shown the immense values for survival and for justice which democracy possesses. But experience also shows that democracy is not practicable in all societies.

Under what circumstances democracy is practicable is a question for empirical inquiry. Here only one or two hypotheses will be suggested. Locke's theory indicates one necessary condition: the bulk of the people must recognize and accept the Law of Reason; they must be men of good will. They must have some sense of their duty to themselves and to others and must follow that sense in their interpretation of what government ought and ought not to do.

But if this were the only type of agreement among the people, the process of discussion in a democracy would be weighed down with an impossible burden. There are many different sets of political and social institutions in which the Law of Reason can be embodied. Some we can judge to be superior to others; many are morally of equal value, and yet incompatible with one another in a single society. The economic system alone severely limits the types of institution and personality which can flourish. Today the captain of industry and the family business may be passing into the limbo which already harbors knight and guildsman, manor and commune. But economic limits are not the only, not even the most important, limits. There are many other causes for a man being born too late or too soon. "The great arc along which all possible human behaviors are distributed," writes Ruth Benedict, "is far too immense and too full of contradictions for any one culture to utilize even any considerable portion of it."[15]

If a democracy is to succeed, there must be more than good will and a process of discussion. The people must also substantially agree on some more concrete interpretation of the Law of Reason as it is to apply to their society. By and

large they must share the same view of the types of creative
activity which are to be allowed and encouraged and the same
view of the types of service to others which the state may
oblige its members to perform. The Law of Reason must be
embodied in some agreed system of Fundamental Law. Or to
use the language of the idealists: the democratic state must be
a community in the sense that the purposes of its members
must be informed by what A. D. Lindsay calls "a standard of
the common life." [16]

It is a harsh and dangerous necessity that the Law of
Reason must be embodied in a system of Fundamental Law.
It is harsh because the Fundamental Law by committing the
society to certain types of self-realization thereby excludes or
greatly burdens other types of self-realization. The state may
preserve liberty for certain types of self-realization, but it
cannot preserve liberty in general. Yet, and here is the danger,
men who happen to be satisfied with the institutions of their
place and time are strongly inclined to think that the liberty
which is liberty to them is liberty to all and that the Fundamental Law protecting that liberty is identical with the
Natural Law. [17] They fail to realize that even a liberal society
has its bias, its peculiar perspective, and that even a democratic
government is not truly an "impartial judge." They may,
therefore, fail to consult their own sense of the imperative of
reason, when it would indicate a practical opportunity for
creative advance.

*Conclusion*  What use then is the philosophy of creative advance to the student of government or to the citizen?

First, from this philosophy an ethics of politics can be
derived. The ethics of humanity states the duty of man. It
therefore indicates the end to be served by all human institutions. That duty and that end is to promote rational self-
realization among all men.

This is an honored formula in ethical and political theory.
But those who use it do not always make clear what they

mean by self-realization. A great value of Dewey's analysis of intelligent inquiry in particular, and rational experience in general, is that it gives a clear, though abstract, meaning to the term. Whitehead's metaphysics goes on to illuminate the relations of creative intelligence with a kindred universe and also, if my interpretation is correct, that stage of experience from which men derive their sense of obligation. From these insights, we can derive a political theory based on reason and directed toward liberty.

For this ethics of politics is essentially liberal. Its central value is the creativity of the individual soul. It directs our attention to that moment when novelty ingresses into the process of human experience. But that moment is a moment of solitude for the individual. The materials from which the insight of such a moment arise are derived from society and nature. That insight will be relevant to those materials. But the insight itself is a new fact in the world, a novel actual entity, occurring only in the process of this soul. In this sense, it is the spontaneous creation, the free act, of the soul. It exhibits the inner liberty of man.

And such a moment is not only fact; it is also purpose. Modestly or profoundly, it alters the plans, the intended behavior, of the individual, giving some new bent to the path of his unique personal adventure. Precisely because it is new as thought and as action, such a creative moment cannot arise if the individual's life is governed by the commands of a tyrant or the rules of inflexible custom. A life which is wholly planned from a center outside the individual cannot be creative. Man is internally free; therefore, he ought to be externally free.

Liberty is not merely that condition in which men refrain from interfering with one another. It is more than merely being let alone. Human creativity does not operate in a vacuum, but in intimate interaction with society and nature. It may be heightened by the presence of certain conditions and strained and frustrated by their absence. Poverty may oppress the soul as severely as tyranny, and the lack of education may be more stultifying than poverty or force. Just what positive conditions will be most beneficial to the creative advance of a society or and individual must be decided on empirical grounds. Liberty in this respect will be defined differently from age to age, and from one society to another. The fact to which this ethics points is that liberty requires appropriate external conditions and that the duty of men to one another is to try to provide these conditions.

Yet these conditions are external. That is, through individual and collective effort, men can provide the conditions necessary for creative advance. So much they can plan. But by definition the act of creativity itself cannot be planned. The scientific inquirer can be provided with his instruments and laboratory. He can be educated in the knowledge and technique of his science and incited to research. So much others can do for him. But the discoveries he makes, the new hypotheses he conceives and confirms, these things he must produce by himself. Similarly, in a society men can provide one another with the conditions of liberty, positive and negative. But the creative use of these conditions depends on the individual in his solitude. Men cannot plan the creative acts of one another. To try to do so would be as futile as trying to plan the discoveries of the scientific inquirer and could only stultify the essential spirit of man. The most, and the best, men can do for one another is to make their society free.

This ethics of politics, then, has content and meaning and can be used in deliberating the concrete issues of modern government. Yet it is not committed to the legal structure or economic system or customs of any particular age. The philosophy on which this ethics is based emphasizes the relativity of all institutions. No man, no institution, no government, can satisfy the moral imperative. Relative to perfection, all fall far short. The gulf between the ideal and the actual is never bridged, although the duty of man is continually to try to bridge it.

Institutions are not only ethically relative, but also histori-cally relative. Only in a certain historical environment does an institution work to produce the consequences expected of it. When that environment changes, the institution must also be changed. In the course of history, familiar forms and procedures will from time to time produce strange and un-wanted results. Men must be prepared to recognize such changes and to alter their institutions accordingly. Historic-ally no forms of government can be eternal; morally none ought to be eternal.

This ethics states an ideal in highly abstract terms. That ideal by itself does not enable a man to decide which of several alternative institutions or reforms of government he ought to support. To make this decision he must interrogate experience. The question is: According to the evidence, which of these alternatives will promote a less imperfect realization of the ideal? He may have to reject a more attractive alterna-tive because it is improbable. The more acutely aware he is of the demands of reason, the more deeply dissatisfied he will be with the compromises forced on him by practicality. But it is his duty to be rationally empirical, that is, scientific.

For this ethics and the religious insight from which it de-rives do not conflict with political science, or with any kind of science. On the contrary, this ethics and this faith alone makes sense of science, saving the pursuit of truth from the attacks of the skeptic and the defeatist. This ethics does indi-cate the end or purpose of science. It states the central prob-lem of human practice: What means will more efficiently pro-mote rational self-realization? Similarly, it states for political science the central problem: What means will more efficiently promote and protect liberty? But this ethics does not pre-judge the finds of empirical inquiry into these questions. It leaves the realm of means entirely to science, and that is the only realm with which science as such is concerned. This ethics is not a scientific ethics—such a phrase is a contradiction in terms. It is rather the ethics of science.

Scientific inquiry cannot be hostile to rational self-realization because in essence they are the same operation. Scientific inquiry is not a form of operation confined to the professional pursuit of knowledge by men in laboratories and research centers. As Dewey continually emphasizes, the principles of scientific inquiry have a much wider application. They are the principles of creative growth of knowledge and purpose. The inquiry of the professional scientist is simply one of the more brilliant achievements of creative intelligence. The vocation of man is the pursuit of truth; science is one calling within this larger vocation.

To try to defend science in particular, or rational empiricism in general, may seem academic, that is, something which only a few people would care to do and which really need not be done. The problem can take a dry and technical form, as, for instance, when stated as the problem of induction. But what I have tried to show in this book is that the problem of defending rational empiricism not only adumbrates the great problems of human destiny, but also impinges on the decisions of everyday life. Every step you take, every word you utter, every vote you cast, assumes some sort of answer to what I have called the problem of purpose.

It has been said that the central problem of our age is fatality: the loss of control over our destiny. There is a certain terror which must seize a man when he considers the choices he is obliged to make as a citizen in the modern world. The experts and the leaders present their conflicting policies to the people. Upon a right choice depends the difference between war and peace, prosperity and depression, progress and decay and collapse. Yet each policy, at the best, complex, closely reasoned and buttressed with facts, is an airy bridge of the imagination, arching off in a different direction into the dark of an unknown future. Each wants to be, even pretends to be, the future. Each is only a construction of the mind, a mere probability, a plan and a purpose. Where can a man find the confidence to set foot on any one of these ethereal structures?

Prejudice by blinding him may give him that confidence. And as the facts force upon him the doubts of irrationalism, prejudice can protect confidence by becoming fanaticism. A sense of humor may lead to a more civilized response. For the contrast between fact, what is and will be, and theory, what men think and expect, is a comic contrast. But seeing the joke will not fortify the heart and gives over  leadership to the fanatics.

The solution which I have tried to suggest embodies the humility of the cynic, but not his defeatism and loss of nerve. It includes the decision of the fanatic, but not his pride. It draws a firm and abiding confidence in reason from a faith which reason itself reveals.

# NOTES

## CHAPTER ONE

1. A. N. Whitehead, *Adventures of Ideas* (New York: The Macmillan Company, 1933), p. 64.
2. Ludwig Wittgenstein, *Tractatus Logico-Philosophicus* (New York: Harcourt, Brace & Company, 1933), p. 109.
3. A. N. Whitehead, *Science and the Modern World* (New York: The Macmillan Company, 1935), p. 35.
4. For a clear and penetrating exposition of the meanings of rationalism and irrationalism in agreement with the use of the terms in this book, see Francis S. Haserot, "The Meaning of Rationalism," *The Journal of Philosophy*, vol. XLIV, No. 8 (April 10, 1947).
5. Quoted in Karl Mannheim, *Ideology and Utopia* (New York: Harcourt, Brace and Company, 1936). p. 121, note.

## CHAPTER TWO

1. *Ideology and Utopia* (Harcourt, Brace and Company), p. 91.
2. *Ideology and Utopia*, p. 3
3. *Ideology and Utopia*, pp. 105 and 106.
4. Pendleton Herring, *Presidential Leadership* (New York: Farrar and Rinehart, Inc., 1940), p. 117.
5. *Ideology and Utopia*, p. 132.
6. *Ideology and Utopia*, pp. 169-170.
7. *Ideology and Utopia*, p. 170.
8. J. S. Mill, *A System of Logic*, Book III, ch. viii, par. 2
9. *Logic*, Book III, ch viii, par. 5.
10. "A high degree of control of conditions is effected by the scientific techniques now available. But there always remains the *theoretical* possibility that *some* conditions which affect the observed phenomenon have not been brought under control. The postulate of a closed existential system is thus a limiting ideal for experimental inquiry. It is a logical ideal which points the direction in which inquiry must move but which cannot be completely attained." John Dewey, *Logic: The Theory of Inquiry* (New York: Henry Holt and Company, 1938), p. 320.
11. See F. C. Mills, *Economic Tendencies in the United States*, (New York: J. J. Little and Ives Company, 1932), *passim*, and especially pp. 44-46, 84-87, 153-160.
12. For example, by Edward H. Chamberlin, *The Theory of Monopolistic Competition* (Cambridge: Harvard University Press, 1933) and Joan Robinson, *The Economics of Imperfect Competition* (1933).

13. A. N. Whitehead, *Process and Reality*, (New York: The Macmillan Company, 1936), p. 311.

14. For a very intelligent attempt to deal with prediction as a problem of the social sciences, see F. H. Knight, *The Ethics of Competition* (London: G. Allen and Uhwin, Ltd., 1936), especially pp. 110-111. Mr. Knight gives a neat statement of "the paradox, that if the world is always the same there is no problem of prediction, while if it is not the same, prediction is impossible."

15. "We have no certainty as to foreseeing the future. We do not know whether the predictions of complicated theories, such as the quantum theory or the theory of albumen molecules, will turn out to be true; we do not even know whether the simplest posits concerning our immediate future will be confirmed—whether they concern the sun's rising or the persistence of the conditions of our personal environment. There is no principle of philosophy to warrant the reliability of such predictions; that is our answer to all attempts made within the history of philosophy to procure for us such certainty, from Plato, through all varieties of theology, to Descartes and Kant." Hans Reichenbach, *Experience and Prediction* (Chicago: University of Chicago Press, 1938), p. 401.

16. For a clear and penetrating study of the theory of induction in connection with probability theory, see Donald Williams, *The Ground of Induction* (Cambridge: The Harvard University Press, 1947). While presenting his own solution (see below, n. 20), Mr. Williams summarizes much of the recent discussion of the problem.

17. "To an inhabitant of Central Africa, fifty years ago," wrote Mill in 1843, "no fact probably appeared to rest upon more uniform experience than this, that all human beings are black. To Europeans, not many years ago, the proposition, All swans are white, appeared an equally unequivocal instance of uniformity in the course of nature." *Logic*, Book III, ch. iii, par. 2.

18. It is easy to ridicule "the quest for certainty" and to demand that we refuse to claim certainty for anything we know. But to meet this demand, if possible, requires at least a revolution in our use of the terms "to know" and "knowledge." For does not the notion of knowledge inevitably carry the notion of certainty with it? When you say you know something, do you not mean that you are certain about a belief, even if you only mean, as you usually do, that you are certain about the degree of probability which some proposition has? See J. M. Keynes, *A Treatise on Probability* (London: Macmillan and Company, Ltd., 1921), ch. ii, "Probability in Relation to the Theory of Knowledge," where he writes in part: "The highest degree of rational belief, which is termed *certain* rational belief, corresponds to *knowledge*. We may be said to know a thing when we have a certain rational belief in it, and *vice versa*" (p. 10).

19. Consider what would have to be known in order to satisfy Mill's definition of a cause. He writes: "The cause, then, philosophically speaking, is the sum total of the conditions, positive and *negative*, taken together; the whole of the contingencies of every description, which being realized, the consequent *invariably* follows." (My italics.) *Logic*, Book III, ch. v, par. 3.

20. In *The Ground of Induction*, Donald Williams develops a purely logical argument in support of inductive reasoning. Briefly, he he argues that according to the mathematical law of large numbers, most "samples" match their "populations" in composition; that, therefore, it is probable that any particular "largish" sample on which an induction is based will match its population. However, he insists that this does not mean that we can be certain that "by persistently believing in highly probable propositions we shall be right more frequently than if we believed improbable ones." (See ch. iii, "The Maturity of the Chances.") He holds that it is more reasonable, indeed logically necessary, to believe probabilities, even though we know they tell us nothing certain about the future.

Williams' argument does not meet the problem of purpose. The essence of knowledge as purpose is its reference to the future. If you cut off purposive knowledge from its reference to the future, then this knowledge is no longer "credible," i.e., there is no sense in acting on it. (See below, p. 89.) Logic alone cannot justify a man in acting on what may be, and often is, illusion. Only ethics, metaphysics, or religion can do that.

Keynes writes: "The proposition that a course of action guided by the most probable considerations will generally lead to success, is not certainly true and has nothing to recommend it but its probability. The importance of probability can only be derived from the judgment that it is *rational* to be guided by it in action; and a practical dependence on it can only be justified by a judgment that in action we *ought* to act to take some account of it." (*Treatise on Probability*, pp. 322-323.)

## CHAPTER THREE

1. This account of Dewey's ideas is based principally on *Experience and Nature* (New York: W. W. Norton and Co., Inc., 1929), *Human Nature and Conduct* (New York: Henry Holt and Company, 1922), and *Logic: The Theory of Inquiry* (Henry Holt and Company, 1938).

2. See William James, *A Pluralistic Universe* (New York, 1909), ch. vii, "The Continuity of Experience."

3. *Experience and Nature*, p. 367.

4. Ruth Benedict applies a not dissimilar principle to the social sciences in her *Patterns of Culture* (Boston: Houghton Mifflin

# 220

NOTES

Company, 1934). She writes: "The whole, as modern science is insisting in many fields, is not merely the sum of all its parts, but the result of a unique arrangement and inter-relation of the parts that has brought about a new entity . . . Cultures . . . are more than the sum of their traits. We may know all about the distribution of a tribe's form of marriage, ritual dances, and puberty initiations, and yet understand nothing of the culture as a whole which has used these elements to its own purposes" (p. 47). Consequently, she would study a primitive society, not by enumerating the elements of its culture, but by presenting the "configuration" of its culture.

5. *Experience and Nature*, p. 373.
6. "Prediction in science involves a specification of *what steps to take* if we wish to observe a regularity of nature . . . Predicting where a planet will be at a certain date is equivalent to prescribing where to put a telescope at a particular time if we wish to see it. It is, therefore, a recipe for correct conduct." Lancelot Hogben, *Retreat from Reason*, (New York: Random House, 1937), p. 49. Quoted in Dewey's *Logic*, p. 456 n. (Dewey's italics.)
7. In Dewey's *Human Nature and Conduct* the underlying ideas of his *Logic* appear as the fundamental modes of the development of the personality.
8. *Logic: The Theory of Inquiry*, p. 23.
9. *Experience and Nature*, pp. 41-44.
10. *Experience and Nature*, p. 49.
11. See Josiah Royce, *The World and The Individual* (New York, 1899), Supplementary Essay.
12. *Logic: The Theory of Inquiry*, p. 10.

## CHAPTER FOUR

1. A. S. P. Woodhouse (ed.), *Puritanism and Liberty* (London: J. M. Dent and Sons, Ltd., 1938), p. 65.
2. *Leviathan* (London, 1914. Everyman's Library), p. 82.
3. *Utilitarianism, Liberty and Representative Government* (London, 1910. Everyman's Library), p. 6.
4. *General Theory of Value: its meaning and basic principles construed in terms of interest* (New York: Longmans, Green and Company, 1926), p. 124.
5. For example, by Stephen Vincent Benét in his record of the mores of the inhabitants and frequenters of Wingate Hall in his *John Brown's Body* (1928).
6. *The Essays of Montaigne* translated by E. J. Trechman (London, 1927), I, 111 and 112.
7. *Folkways* (Boston, 1906), p. 29.
8. *Patterns of Culture*, p. 237.
9. For the purely moralistic view of natural law, see W. W.

Willoughby's *Ethical Basis of Political Authority* (New York: The Macmillan Company, 1930).

10. Concerning "the use of theories of natural law in judicial decisions on public law" during the post-Civil War period, B. F. Wright, Jr., writes: "Probably the most important developments in American constitutional law since the reign of John Marshall fall within the categories 'due process of law' and 'liberty of contract.' . . . These are theories of right, not utility. Furthermore, they represent the application of old theories of natural law, and particularly of natural rights, to problems never dreamed of by the founding fathers." ("American Interpretations of Natural Law," *The American Political Science Review*, Vol. XX, No. 3: August, 1926, p. 540.)

11. 111 U. S. 746 at 762.

12. For example, by E. S. Corwin, *The Twilight of the Supreme Court* (New Haven: Yale University Press, 1934), pp. 77-78, and ch. ii, *passim*; and by Robert E. Cushman, *Leading Constitutional Decisions* (New York: F. S. Crofts and Company, 1937; sixth edition), p. 95.

13. The first issue of *The Nation* appeared on July 6, 1865; then and for long thereafter, under the editorship of E. L. Godkin, it preached laisser-faire. See I. F. Stone on Godkin, in *The Nation* for February 10, 1940, pp. 158-161.

14. F. C. Mills, *Economic Tendencies in the United States*, especially pp. 44-46, 84-87, 153-160.

15. In *Morehead, Warden, v. New York ex rel. Tipaldo* (298 U. S. 587). Quoting indirectly from the Adkins case (261 U. S. 525), the Court said: "The right to make contracts about one's affairs is a part of the liberty protected by the due process clause. Within this liberty are provisions of contracts between employer and employee fixing the wages to be paid . . . Legislative abridgement of that freedom can only be justified by the existence of exceptional circumstances."

## CHAPTER FIVE

1. *Fundamental Principles of the Metaphysic of Ethics*, Translated by T. K.Abbott (London; tenth edition.), p. 4.

2. See the debates in the council of Cromwell's Army in A. S. P. Woodhouse's *Puritanism and Liberty*. On the meaning of the term "reason" at that time, see Woodhouse's Introduction, especially pp. 94-95.

3. *Fundamental Principles of the Metaphysic of Ethics*, p. 46.

4. My translation from C. E. Vaughan's edition of the *Contrat Social* (London, 1918), p. 14.

5. *Experience and Nature*, p. 178-179. For Dewey's views on communication, see ch. v of that work.

6. *Community: A Sociological Study* (New York: The Macmillan Company, 1928), p. 104.
7. *Ethical Studies* (London, 1876), p. 204.
8. A phrase used by Bosanquet to describe J. S. Mill's view of human nature. See B. Bosanquet, *The Philosophical Theory of the State* (London: Macmillan and Company, 1923), p. 57.
9. See Dewey's *Human Nature and Conduct,* especially Part IV, Section IV.
10. By the late G. H. Palmer, quoted in W. E. Hocking's *Types of Philosophy* (New York: Charles Scribner's Sons, 1929), p. 148.
11. The terms "real will" and "actual will" are from Bosanquet's discussion in his *Philosophical Theory of the State,* pp. 110-113 and *passim.*

## CHAPTER SIX

1. There was a strong trace of this kind of thinking among the Guild Socialists. See, e.g., Arthur J. Penty's *Old Worlds for New* (London, 1918), ". . . we seek to replace existing society by a society based upon the civilization of the past," p. 185, and *Guilds, Trade and Argiculture* (London, 1921), ". . . the reconstruction of agriculture must take precedence over all other industries," p. 78.
2. Rudolf Stammler, *Theory of Justice* (New York: The Macmillan Company, 1925).
3. The Hegelians are more likely to appreciate this point than the Kantians. See, for instance, the Hegelian theory of Josef Kohler's *Philosophy of Law* (Boston, 1914). Kohler holds that the function of law is to promote "in the first place, an intensive development of the individual with the highest possible training of all the mental powers; and, in the second, steady cohesion in order that humanity may not fall apart into individuals . . . an event that would be calamitous" (p. 49).
4. *Fundamental Principles of the Metaphysic of Ethics,* p. 56.
5. It would be worth while to compare the procedures of sincere and successful collective bargaining with the procedures of "comparison-contrast" described by Dewey in his *Logic* as essential modes of scientific problem-solving.
6. *Presidential Leadership,* p. 125.
7. *Essentials of Democracy* (Philadelphia: University of Pennsylvania Press, 1929), pp. 36-37.
8. *Fundamental Principles of the Metaphysic of Ethics,* p. 10.
9. *Human Nature and Conduct,* pp. 267 and 281.

## CHAPTER SEVEN

1. These truths presuppose the continuance of a certain "social epoch." See above, p. 27.

2. Friedrich Engels, *Herr Eugen Dühring's Revolution in Science* (New York: International Publishers; 1939 edition) Marxist Library, XVIII, pp. 125-126.
3. *Anti-Dühring*, p. 44.
4. *TheWorks of Ralph Waldo Emerson* (New York: Tudor Publishing Company), III, 20-21.
5. Karl Marx and Friedrich Engels, *The German Ideology* (New York: International Publishers, 1939), pp. 14-15.
6. *Anti-Dühring*, p. 292.
7. *A Handbook of Marxism*, ed. Emile Burns (New York: International Publishers, 1935), p. 44.
8. Karl Marx, *Capital* (London: J. M. Dent and Sons, Ltd., 1930), I, 169.
9. See Engels, *Feuerbach, the Roots of the Socialist Philosophy* (Chicago, 1908), especially pp. 65-68 and 96-99.
10. *Anti-Dühring*, p. 44
11. *Anti-Dühring*, p. 126.

## CHAPTER EIGHT

1. *The Ecclesiastical History of the English Nation*, By the Venerable Bede (London, 1910; Everyman's Library), p. 91.
2. A. N. Whitehead, *Science and the Modern World*, p. 65.
3. *Science and the Modern World*, p. 35.

## CHAPTER NINE

1. *Logic: The Theory of Inquiry*, p. 23.
2. *Works*, IV, 31.
3. *Works*, IV, 30.
4. *The Dialogues of Plato*, Jowett's translation, (London, 1892; Third Edition), III, 209.
5. *Dialogues*, III, 210.
6. *Dialogues*, III, 207.
7. *Dialogues*, III, 450-451.
8. *Dialogues*, III, 467.
9. *Dialogues*, III, 466.

## CHAPTER TEN

1. Quotations from the Old Testament in this chapter are from *The Holy Scriptures, According to the Masoretic Text* (Philadelphia: Jewish Publication Society of America, 1917).
2. Quotations from the New Testament in this chapter are from the King James Version.
3. *Works*, I, 49-50.
4. Calvin's definition of faith is "une ferme et certaine cognoissance

de la bonne volunté de Dieu envers nous: laquelle estant fondée sur la promesse gratuite donnée en Jesus Christ, est revelée a nostre entendement, et scellée en nostre coeur par le Sainct Esprit." Quoted in H. O. Taylor, *Thought and Expression in the Sixteenth Century* (New York: The Macmillan Company, 1920), I, 414.

5. See F. H. Bradley, *Appearance and Reality* (London, 1930; third edition; ninth impression, corrected), chs. xiii and xiv.

6. My italics.

7. In particular, see Bradley's *Appearance and Reality*, Royce's *World and the Individual*, and Bosanquet's *Principle of Individuality and Value* (London, 1912).

## CHAPTER ELEVEN

1. This exposition of Whitehead's ideas is based principally on *Process and Reality*, *Adventures of Ideas* and *Science in the Modern World*.

2. *The Philosophy of Alfred North Whitehead*, ed. P. A. Schilpp (Evanston: Northwestern University, 1941), pp. 643-661.

3. *Process and Reality*, pp. 34-35.

4. *Adventures of Ideas*, pp. 201-202.

5. Still excepting, of course, the case of negative prehension.

6. "In mere feeling, or immediate presentation, we have the experience of a whole . . . This whole contains diversity, and, on the other hand, is not parted by relations. Such an experience, we must admit, is most imperfect and unstable, and its inconsistencies lead us at once to transcend it. Indeed, we hardly possess it as more than that which we are in the process of losing. But it serves to suggest to us the general idea of a total experience, where will and thought and feeling may all once more be one." (*Appearance and Reality*, pp. 140-141.)

## CHAPTER TWELVE

1. *Process and Reality*, p. 43.

2. *Process and Reality*, p. 166.

3. *Adventures of Ideas*, p. 349.

4. *Process and Reality*, p. 315.

5. *Process and Reality*, p. 245.

6. *Process and Reality*, p. 286.

7. *Experience and Nature*, pp. 311-312.

8. Strictly, a process in which there is destruction is not a concrescence, not a unified growing together. Should we call it, say, an "excrescence"?

9. *Process and Reality*, p. 525.

10. *Works*, IV 46.

11. *Process and Reality*, pp. 524-525.

12. Reinhold Niebuhr, *The Nature and Destiny of Man* (New York: Charles Scribner's Sons, 1946), II, 295.

13. *Process and Reality*, p. 424.

14. Josiah Royce, referring to the views of ancient and medieval students of the problem of evil, wrote: " 'Every evil,' said such students, 'has, as a positive fact in the world of Being, its own internal perfections. Its evil character is due to its relations to other facts that coexist with it in the same world. Even Satan,' said such views, 'is an angel; and even as a fallen angel he has extraordinary perfections of nature, which so far constitute a good. His diabolical quality is due to the misuse of precisely these perfections. The best in wrong setting becomes the worst.' " (*The World and the Individual*, p. 376.)

15. "All historic conceptions of justice will embody some elements which contradict the law of love. The interests of a class, the viewpoint of a nation, the prejudices of an age and the illusions of a culture are consciously and unconsciously insinuated into the norms by which men regulate their common life. They are intended to give one group an advantage over another. Or if that is not their intention, it is at least the unvarying consequence." (Reinhold Niebuhr, *The Nature and Destiny of Man*, II, 256.) On the one hand, there are relative differences in systems of justice and modes of conduct and the duty of man is to choose the better. On the other hand, any such system of justice or mode of conduct will fall far short of the ideal; man dare not overlook "the realities of sin which appear on every new level of virtue." (*The Nature and Destiny of Man*, II, 125.) This contrast is central to the "human situation" as it is delineated by Niebuhr.

## CHAPTER THIRTEEN

1. See above, p. 144.

2. *Dialogues*, I, 571.

3. *Dialogues*, I, 573.

4. *Essays* (First Series New York: Thomas Y. Crowell Company), pp. 195-196.

5. This idea is fundamental to W. E. Hocking's *Meaning of God in Human Experience* (New Haven, 1912); see especially ch. xxii, "The Ontological Argument for the Existence of God."

6. *Appearance and Reality*, p. 124.

7. Hocking writes: "If, then, I discover that my world of nature and self, taken severally or together, falls short of reality, this discovery is due to what I know of reality—not abstractly, but in experience. If I judge this system of nature-and-self to be non-self-sufficient, it is by a knowledge of the self-sufficient; if I condemn, it is by virtue of something in my possession not subject to condemnation; if I criticize and correct, it is by comparison with

226          NOTES

or reference to some present object not subject to criticism and correction. When I perceive myself in this curious relation to the world of physical facts—superior and not superior, creative and unable to create—that play of unrest is due to, and is defining, a simultaneous perception of the object to which this unrest does not apply. The positive content which I give to that absolute object is a report of experience; whatever idea I make of it is an idea derived nowhere but from that experience." (*The Meaning of God in Human Experience*, p. 311.)

8. This feeling has had an immense influence upon history and upon the cultures which man has built, difficult as that influence may be to measure. In Whitehead's *Adventures of Ideas*, this is the theme of the opening chapters, where he is concerned with "the influence exerted by the Platonic and Christian doctrines of the human soul upon the sociological development of the European races."

9. "The essence of rationalism," writes Francis S. Haserot, "is not universal deducibility . . . It is simply this: contradiction and being are incompatible; a statement which is surely innocent enough, but is not without consequences." Concerning the consequences, of "the principle of rationality," he continues: "Since logical possibility and being become synonymous in this view, and contradiction is excluded, it follows that there is something which is, in its nature, self-consistent. For if there is nothing self-consistent, there is no ultimate elimination of contradiction. In other words the non-existence of a self-consistent being would involve a contradiction which would make such non-existence impossible and the existence of such a being necessary. Any self-consistent being is a necessary being. There is then at least one self-consistent and necessary being. Nor could there be two or a plurality of self-consistent beings since they could not be unrelated and their relations would eliminate their respective logical independence. This we take to be the real meaning of the ontological argument which, in other words, says that if contradiction is impossible then there must be some nature, in its own character, non-contradictory, self-consistent and logically perfect." "The Meaning of Rationalism," *Journal of Philosophy*, Vol. XLIV, No. 8 (April 10, 1947).

CHAPTER FOURTEEN

1. See *The Philosophical Theory of the State*, p. 169.
2. *Philosophical Theory*, pp. 162-164.
3. J. S. Mill, *Utilitarianism, Liberty and Representative Government*, pp. 116-117.
4. *Utilitarianism, etc.*, p. 2.
5. *Utilitarianism, etc.*, p. 27.

6. *Utilitarianism, etc.,* p. 117.
7. See above, p. 171.
8. See above, p. 83 and pp. 160-161.
9. See above, p. 21 and p. 85.
10. Quoted above, p. 85.
11. John Locke, *An Essay concerning the True Original, Extent and End of Civil Government,* par. 1.
12. *Ibid.,* par. 1.
13. See Locke's first *Letter Concerning Toleration, passim.*
14. Locke, *An Essay concerning the True Original, Extent and End of Civil Government,* par. 240.
15. Quoted above, p. 58.
16. Lindsay, *The Modern Democratic State,* (London: Oxford University Press, 1943), I, ch.x, "The General Will, or The Standard of the Common Life."
17. See above, pp. 58ff.

# HARVARD POLITICAL STUDIES

A Brief History of the Constitution and Government of Massachusetts. By Louis Adams Frothingham.

The Political Works of James I. Edited by Charles Howard McIlwain.

Politica Methodice Digesta of Johannes Althusius. Edited by Carl Joachim Friedrich.

Municipal Charters. By Nathan Matthews.

A Bibliography of Municipal Government. By William Bennett Munro.

Town Government in Massachusetts, 1630-1930. By John F. Sly.

Interstate Transmission of Electric Power. By Hugh Langdon Elsbree.

American Interpretations of Natural Law. By Benjamin Fletcher Wright, Jr.

Sanctions and Treaty Enforcement. By Payson Sibley Wild, Jr.

Foreign Relations in British Labour Politics. By William Percy Maddox.

Administration of the Civil Service in Massachusetts. By George C. S. Benson.

International Socialism and the World War. By Merle Fainsod.

The President's Control of the Tariff. By John Day Larkin.

Federal Commissioners. By E. Pendleton Herring.

Government Proprietary Corporations in the English-Speaking Countries. By John Thurston.

The Physiocratic Doctrine of Judicial Control. By Mario Einaudi.

The Failure of Constitutional Emergency Powers under the German Republic. By Frederick Mundell Watkins.

The Treasury and Monetary Policy, 1933-1938. By C. Griffith Johnson, Jr.

The Art and Technique of Administration in German Ministries. By Arnold Brecht and Comstock Glaser.

The Political Life of the American Medical Association. By Oliver Garceau.

Nazi Conquest through German Culture. By Ralph F. Bischoff.

The Regulation of Railroad Abandonments. By Charles R. Cherington.

DATE DUE